MARGA

RICHTER

WOMEN COMPOSERS

The short, readable books in the Women Composers series introduce significant women composers to students and general readers and provide a convenient reference for performers and scholars.

Series books treat the broadest range of women composers, combining concise biographical information with a comprehensive survey of works.

A list of books in the series appears at the end of this book.

Marga Richter

Sharon Mirchandani

UNIVERSITY OF
ILLINOIS PRESS
*Urbana, Chicago, and
Springfield*

Manufactured in the United States of America
1 2 3 4 5 C P 5 4 3 2 1
∞ This book is printed on acid-free paper.

Portions of this work were first published in somewhat different format as "The Choral Music of Marga Richter," *Choral Journal* (May 2003): 9–17; and "Marga Richter," in *Women of Influence in Contemporary Music: Nine American Composers*, edited by Michael K. Slayton (Lanham, Md.: Scarecrow Press, 2011), 357–404.

Library of Congress Cataloging-in-Publication Data
Mirchandani, Sharon.
Marga Richter / Sharon Mirchandani.
pages cm.—(Women composers)
Includes bibliographical references and index.
ISBN 978-0-252-03731-3 (hardcover : alk. paper)
ISBN 978-0-252-07891-0 (pbk. : alk. paper)
1. Richter, Marga. 2. Composers—United States—Biography.
3. Women composers—United States—Biography. I. Title.
ML410.R49235M37 2012
780.92—dc23 2012037197
[B]

To Dilip

CONTENTS

ILLUSTRATIONS

PREFACE

I FIRST BECAME AWARE OF Marga Richter's music in 2003 when I was preparing to teach a course on women in music and listened to the audio cassette for Diane Jezic's *Women Composers: The Lost Tradition Found*. I found Richter's *Landscapes of the Mind II* for violin and piano to be quite engaging and wanted to know more about the composer. I soon discovered that she was a highly skilled composer of a large body of instrumental and vocal works that are attractive to the listener, challenging to the performer, and exhibit superior craftsmanship. I found her particularly impressive as there have been few women composers of large-scale orchestral music until quite recently.

Much of Richter's music has been performed and frequently commissioned by prominent artists (including soprano Jessye Norman; pianists Menahem Pressler and William Masselos; conductors Carlos Surinach, Izler Solomon, Stanislaw Skrowaczewski, Gerard Schwarz, Marin Alsop, and JoAnn Falletta; violist Walter Trampler; and violinist Daniel Heifetz), while reviews of the performances have been consistently filled with much praise for her compositions. Her orchestral works have been performed by more than fifty orchestras including the Atlanta Symphony Orchestra, the Minnesota Orchestra, the Milwaukee Symphony Orchestra, and the Civic Orchestra of Chicago. She has received awards and grants from the American Society of Composers and Publishers, the National Endowment for the Arts, the Martha Baird Rockefeller fund, and the National Federation of Music Clubs. Most of her music has been published—much of it recorded and virtually all of it performed. In 1975 she received a contract from a major publisher, Carl Fischer.

Marga Richter and I have spoken on the phone hundreds of times since 2003. We have also met in person numerous times beginning in February 2005 when I stayed with her for several days at her Long Island home. Since then I have visited and spoken with her periodically discussing music, composition, women's roles, raising children, life, relationships, and religion. But mostly music. Music is her main identity. At the age of eighty-five she is still an active composer, and she continues to have premieres of new works.

The documentation and consideration of Marga Richter's music is the most important aspect of this book. Her music, composed over much of the twentieth century and into the twenty-first, is expressive and interesting, frequently inspired by high-quality U.S., Irish/English, and Asian images or texts. Especially notable are her large-scale works for orchestra: *Blackberry Vines and Winter Fruit*, *Landscapes of the Mind I*, *Spectral Chimes/Enshrouded Hills*, *Out of Shadows and Solitude* and her triple concerto: *Variations and Interludes on Themes from Monteverdi and Bach*; her chamber opera *Riders to the Sea*; her *Sonata* and her *Requiem* for piano; and her song cycles *Testament* and *Dew-drops on a Lotus Leaf*. The nature, origins, and first performances for most of her works are detailed, and many of the numerous reviews are included. The reference section of the book also contains complete lists of her works and recordings. Richter's musical aesthetics and style are described, particularly her early dissonant style, her rejection of the twelve-tone method, her layered textures and ostinatos, and her more tonal later works. I intend for this explication of her music to offer a more complete view of the musical styles used by U.S. twentieth-century composers.

This book is also the first complete biography of Marga Richter and portrays in detail Richter's upbringing, early training, and musical career over the course of the twentieth century and into the twenty-first. A theme in the book is Richter's relationship to feminism. While Richter does not like the phrase "woman composer" and never called herself a feminist, I do believe it is important to have a place, like this University of Illinois Press series on women composers, in which to focus specifically on women composers in order to add to and challenge our understanding of gender roles. The effects on Richter's career of social differences, marriage, children, widowhood, and her own understanding of her gender role are explored throughout this book. Her life is one example of how a woman's life tends to develop on a different schedule in a different way than a man's life, often making it harder for a woman to receive recognition for her work. The seven chapters progress chronologically and depict the different phases in her life: "The Early Years: 1926–1951," "Modern Dance and the MGM Recordings: 1951–1960," "Fragments: 1960s," "Landscapes: 1970s," "Expansion: 1980s," "Culmination: 1990s," and "Blooming: 2000s–Present." Richter's greatest public successes occurred mostly during two phases: the early 1950s before she had children, and again in the 1970s after her children were becoming more independent.

I have enjoyed getting to know Marga Richter. She is young-minded and independent, takes an hour-long brisk walk in the hills around her Huntington Harbor home most afternoons, makes homemade cranberry sauce, has large bells and her own artwork on her walls, collects old blue mason jars, and plays her vintage Steinway grand piano. Marga Richter also likes language—grammar, crossword puzzles, wit, jokes, and wordplay. She is funny! She is still composing, learning (including the Sibelius music notation software), and actively involved with musical life. She is kind, and, most surprising to me, still able to fall in love. It is my hope that this book will increase our knowledge of her musical contributions and inspire young composers and artists by documenting her life and music.

ACKNOWLEDGMENTS

I WOULD LIKE TO THANK Rider University for supporting my work with a research leave, several summer fellowships, and an intellectually stimulating work environment. I am most appreciative to the Talbott and Moore librarians for their steady advice and assistance. I also benefited greatly from counsel by the members of my own Music Composition, History and Theory Department, and the members of Rider's Gender and Sexuality Studies Program. Numerous fellow colleagues and scholars have inspired and encouraged this work, and I would especially like to thank Nancy Wicklund and Judy Johnston. I greatly appreciate the skill and professionalism of senior acquisitions editor Laurie Matheson, the expertise of copyeditor Deborah Oliver, and the valuable advice I received from the anonymous readers for the University of Illinois Press.

Richter's children, Michael Skelly and Maureen Skelly Raj, were wonderfully supportive of this project, along with numerous performers of her works. I would especially like to thank Marga Richter for her artistry, generous hospitality, and patience with my many questions. Thanks also to my family for their constant encouragement: Dilip, Maia, and Milan.

MARGA RICHTER

1 The Early Years
1926–1951

From the beginning I used all twelve tones of the chromatic scale as equals, although at times one tone might be more important than the others, and the music is essentially melodic. I recently looked at one of my early songs and was totally surprised to find that the piano part contains harmonic and melodic elements that I am still using—passages using only consecutive 7ths and 9ths, including a very dissonant passage in minor 9ths with a type of inner figuration which has remained as an element of my later style. This rather amazed me since at that time I had heard very little contemporary music (no Schoenberg, Stravinsky or Bartók for instance) and had played none.

Marga Richter, 1979, quoted in LePage, *Women Composers*

ON OCTOBER 21, 1926, Florence Marga Richter was born in Reedsburg, Wisconsin, the heart of the American Midwest. The strong musical upbringing Marga Richter received, combined with the midwestern values of hard work and independence, was the foundation out of which she grew to compose a large, distinctive body of works over her lifetime. Her music is primarily in the style and genres of Western art music and at times draws inspiration from distinctly U.S., Irish/English, and Asian sources. Nearly all of her music, including her orchestral works, has received performances. It has been rare for women to compose large-scale orchestral compositions, so her accomplishment in this area is particularly impressive. This book's exploration of her life and works sheds light on Marga Richter's contributions to women's history and America's musical history.

Roots

Richter's mother, Inez Chandler Richter (née Davis) (1885–1956), was an American soprano whose operatic career was solely in Germany, just before, during, and after World War I. She married William Chandler by the time they were listed in the 1910 census in Minneapolis, Hennepin County, Minnesota. On March 1, 1913, they went to Germany, where Will served in the diplomatic corps, and Inez studied voice with the renowned Madame Schoen-René, who prepared her for her Berlin debut recital in 1916. Marga recounts that just before the concert Will Chandler became ill with pneumonia, worsened by the climate in northern Germany. His doctor recommended that the couple decamp to southern Germany, but he refused to uproot Inez before her big debut. Three days before the concert, he died. Madame Schoen-René assumed Inez would cancel. Inez refused to do so, saying, "This man gave up his life for me. I will honor him by dedicating this concert to him." Inez then returned, presumably with Chandler's body,

1. Inez Chandler in Boccaccio *as a peasant boy, ca. 1920.*

2. *Inez and Paul Richter (Marga's parents), ca. 1945.*

to the United States and went to live with her parents in Reedsburg. In 1920 she returned to Germany to resume her operatic career.

Richter's father, Paul Richter, was a captain in the German army during World War I. According to Marga, upon returning home to Einbeck in 1921 from captivity in Persia, he ventured out to the local opera house specifically to see and hear Inez Chandler, the soprano he was told was too "snooty" to mingle with the local lads. He fell in love on the spot, went backstage to meet her, stayed four hours, and "sealed the deal." (He was a born salesman, making his career as an insurance agent, as an assessor, and running a local newspaper.) They were married in 1922 and immediately came to the United States and settled in Reedsburg, Wisconsin, where Marga and her older sister Rena were born. In 1927 the family moved to Minneapolis, where her brother Paul was born in 1929.[1] In 1932 they moved once again, to Robbinsdale, a suburb of Minneapolis, where they stayed until 1943.

Marga's paternal grandfather, Richard Richter, was a composer, municipal orchestra conductor, and music teacher in Einbeck, Germany. Though she never met him, she did play one of his piano pieces, *Unter den Linden*. He refused to teach music to his own children, but Marga's father taught himself to play the piano and had a lifelong passion for music. Marga met her paternal grandmother just once when she visited the United States and stayed with Marga's mother and father for a time. Marga's maternal grandparents were farmers of Canadian-Welsh origin and eventually moved from Reedsburg into the Richter home in Robbinsdale.

Marga's mother, Inez, was extremely important as a role model for Marga, both personally and musically. While Inez raised her three children (who were born when she was thirty-eight, forty-one, and forty-four), she continued her pro-

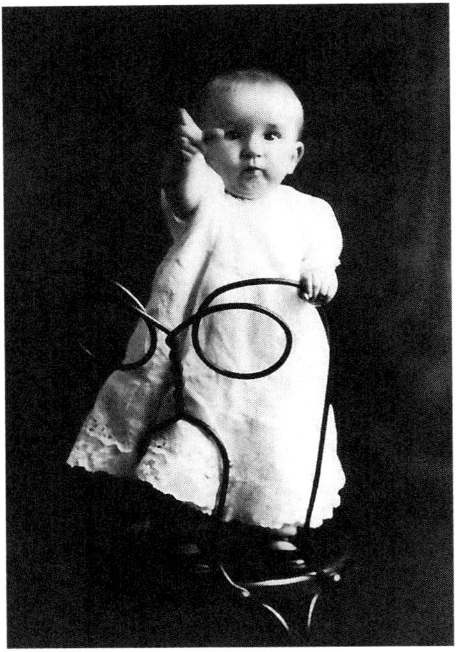

3. Marga Richter conducting, ca. 1927.

fessional career, giving a number of recitals, teaching voice, both at the University of Minnesota and privately, conducting a women's choral group for a time, and performing as soloist at the Second Church of Christ, Scientist, in Minneapolis. Marga recalls her mother being in demand for singing at funerals, because when she sang hymns she moved and comforted the listeners. Marga feels this may have been her mother's greatest gift to her . . . the belief that music should reach the hearts of one's listeners, and that it must communicate. Inez Chandler's last high-profile engagement was as soloist in an all-Wagner program with the Minneapolis Symphony Orchestra and Eugene Ormandy on March 18, 1934, which Marga remembers attending. Marga reflected, "I do not remember the music . . . I only have a visual memory of how she looked on the big stage, attired in a black velvet gown with a bodice encrusted with rhinestones, which I thought were diamonds."[2]

Marga's father, Paul, also strongly influenced her musical and personal life. Although dissuaded from pursuing a career in music, he had enough skill as a musician to conduct a choir in Reedsburg. Marga recalls that he had a good enough tenor voice to participate in the impromptu musicales he and Inez hosted, where

4. Inez Richter with Marga, brother Paul, and sister Rena, ca. 1934.

the two of them took turns as accompanist, as soloist, or in duets. He also often played Beethoven's *Moonlight Sonata* to help his children drift off to sleep. ("His tempos in the faster movements were closer to a turtle's than a hare's.") His love of music and knowledge of the great German romantic composers, along with the poets and philosophers of that era defined his life. He almost never missed the Saturday afternoon radio broadcasts of the Metropolitan Opera and the Sunday broadcasts of the New York Philharmonic. If the opera was by Wagner, his favorite, he insisted on silence throughout the house. She recalls, "We didn't dare even walk through the living room."[3] The psychological and philosophical underpinnings of Wagner's slowly unfolding music may have been a subconscious influence on Marga's own music.

Another aspect of the influence of Marga's mother was her leaving her Baptist roots and becoming a Christian Scientist, after the family moved from Reedsburg to Minneapolis. Marga's father had been Lutheran, but left the church after he resisted taking baby Marga out in the cold Wisconsin winter to be baptized and was told by the minister that she would go to hell without it. He never set foot in a church again, but acquiesced with his wife's choice of Christian Science. Marga considered herself a Christian Scientist and attended Sunday school regularly until the mandatory cut-off age of twenty. She went to church services for a few months after that and then gave up all organized religion. Her early experiences did however shape many of her attitudes throughout life. She finds beauty in nature all around her and tries to think good thoughts and keep her health up. She believes the lack of strict orthodoxy and rituals in the Christian Science church may have fostered her lifelong penchant for following her own muse in her creative and personal life. She also considers the sexes as equals; perhaps this is from the Christian Science understanding of God as both mother and father. Christian Scientists eschew drugs or surgery for medical treatment and instead emphasize healing through prayer, akin to relieving the stresses that may cause disease, and she recalls trying to cure headaches with thought as a teenager. Though she did not continue this as an adult, she recalls not knowing quite how to swallow an aspirin when she was first offered one by a fellow Juilliard student. She never saw a doctor until her 1952 bout with pneumonia, and in her eighties is in robust good health, taking no medication. She believes in a creator, but considers an afterlife unknowable and plans to be cremated.

Both of Marga's parents instilled in her the belief that she could follow her dreams and supported her musical endeavors in every way.

Early Musical Experiences

When asked about her earliest musical training, Richter recalled:

> My earliest, I was told about. I don't remember it. I was three. My sister was taking piano lessons and practicing and when she'd play a wrong note or hesitate . . . I was sitting on the floor with my dolls . . . I'd sing out the proper note. And that's when my parents said, in effect, "let's take a look at *this* kid."[4]

So, by age four, Richter began to take piano lessons from Mary Dillingham in Minneapolis. From her she learned much about musical phrasing, dynamics, rhythm, and the importance of playing with "feeling." Because of her good ear, and because much of the learning at first was by rote, Richter easily memorized every piece. The downside of this method was that she did not become a good sight reader, a fact she definitely regrets. When Richter was ten, Dillingham was seriously injured in a car accident and was unable to continue teaching. Richter then continued piano lessons with Irene Hellner, who became a close friend of the family.

Richter learned the standard European piano repertoire of the day, with emphasis on Bach, Haydn, Mozart, and Beethoven. She specifically recalls playing the following works: Bach: Preludes and Fugues, English Suites, the Italian Concerto, and Partitas; sonatas by Haydn, Mozart, Beethoven, and Schubert; Schumann *Arabesque No. 1*; Chopin: waltzes, mazurkas, preludes, polonaises, ballades, and études; Grieg: Concerto in A Minor; Rachmaninoff: Preludes in G Minor and C Minor; Debussy: *Reverie*; Griffes: *Clouds*; Bartók: *Mikrokosmos*; Shostakovich: Prelude in E Minor; and Soler: *Fandango*.

Though she had no theory or composition lessons, Richter began to compose on her own at age twelve. Richter believes that the desire to compose came from an innate longing to express her ineffable emotions, especially in regard to her emotional attachments to the significant people in her life. As a teenager, she experienced three intense "crushes" on teachers and friends, and used music performance and composition to garner their attention and ultimately their admiration.

The first of these was for her seventh- and eighth-grade English and science teacher, Mary Howell (later Brinkman). Richter recalls, "In order to bring myself to her attention I started to affect a very troubled demeanor when around her, which eventually had the desired result: she asked me what was wrong and I confided in her that I had found papers at home that indicated I was adopted. She acted appropriately shocked and sympathetic. I soon had to admit this was not true, but now we had a special bond."[5] Howell then took a special interest in Richter, admiring her musical accomplishments, which included a birthday song called "I'm Thinking of You" that Richter wrote for her. (The song, a very conventional ditty, did double duty when Richter sent the same song to her cousin Helen several months later. "Always one to extract full value from an idea," quips Richter.) When Howell announced that she was leaving to be married, Richter was devastated at the thought of never seeing her again. She remembers, "I poured my deep feelings of impending loss into my interpretation of Goddard's *Second Barcarolle*, which I was going to play at a piano recital in Minneapolis on the last day of the school year. I wanted to play this *for her* so she would understand how much I loved her and she had agreed to come. The afternoon of the concert, she invited me to come to her apartment and told me she simply did not have the time, because she was packing to leave immediately. I was crushed. I went home and cried for a very long time."[6]

As it turned out, the relationship continued. They exchanged letters, and Howell, now Brinkman, sent Richter a pair of white mittens embroidered with colorful flowers for Christmas of that year (1940) and notified her of the impending birth of her first child (1941), for whom Richter composed her second piece, another song for which she wrote the words as well, and sent it to her. "It was probably called *Lullaby*. The piece has been lost, and I cannot remember all of it, but the opening theme marked the beginning of what I feel is my personal, original style: tonality immediately gone awry. The pitches are C–F–G–G♯–A–F♯–D♯."[7]

In 1943 when Richter left Minnesota to study music in New York, she saw Brinkman one more time. Richter contacted Brinkman, knowing she lived in a suburb of Chicago, to ask if they could see each other during Richter's layover in that city. Brinkman graciously invited her to stay with her in lieu of a hotel. Richter was overjoyed to see Brinkman and to meet the child for whom she had written the lullaby. After a few more letters and Brinkman's move to Denver, Colorado, they lost touch. Sixty-seven years later, at age eight-one, Richter used the Brinkman lullaby melody (revised) in her piano piece *March Berserk*.

Irving Boekelheide was the second teacher to play a significant role in her life. He joined the faculty at Richter's high school in 1940 and taught mathematics and directed the chorus. Richter's aptitude in his algebra class brought her to his attention, and he soon became interested in her as a musician, and as a person. He, himself, was a composer and violinist, and he asked Richter to perform his *Theme with Four Variations* on a school assembly program. She recalls:

> It was the first contemporary music I had ever played, full of changing meters, jazzy rhythms, slightly dissonant harmonies, and formally quixotic. I lost the music in a fire [see chapter 2], but when we reconnected, due to my sleuthing in 1995, he sent me a copy. I was amazed to find that this piece had made an indelible impression on my subconscious musical mind, to the point that I unknowingly used a few of the melodic and rhythmic fragments in my own music, years later. This performance definitely created a bond between us.[8]

He further influenced Richter's musical development by bringing a record player into a classroom after school to play orchestral music for her. Franck's *Symphony in D Minor* was her favorite.

Boekelheide also arranged for her to attend the Minneapolis Symphony concerts (Dimitri Mitropoulos, conductor). Her parents allowed her to go by herself on public transportation, since he offered to drive her home. She remembers:

> These concerts, at which I first heard great orchestral music and soloists live, including the premiere of the Shostakovich Seventh Symphony and Rachmaninoff playing his second piano concerto, were a great source of inspiration and joy. And I was by then totally "in love" with Boekelheide. And, it would seem, his interest in me was not totally platonic. After the last concert of the season, rather than take me directly home, we drove around for awhile,

> and he made three responses I have never forgotten, to something I must have said: "The only thing wrong with you is you are only fourteen"; "If you were older I would be rougher in my talk"; "I am only sorry there are only eleven more weeks of you."[9]

The relationship, which remained innocent, was a heady experience and further exposed Richter to the act of composition and to high-caliber performances. She recalls that working with him on his music made composition seem like a normal thing to do.

Richter continues:

> As I had with Howell, when I knew he [Boekelheide] was not returning to the school in the fall, I made my feelings of sadness known to him by playing Liszt's *Consolation No. 3* for him on the last day of school in the music room. I thought I would never see him again. Unexpectedly, we kept in touch by telephone through the fall. In October he invited me to go with him to St. Paul to play his *Theme with Four Variations* for his composition teacher, Donald Ferguson. After I played, we were offered tea. Asked if I would like a cup, I demurred and said I would just like the lemon. This attempt at humor was met with stony-faced incomprehension. As a Christian Scientist, I had never had either tea or coffee. Our host took me seriously and I, blushing, had to decline the proffered wedge. I saw Boekelheide once more, probably in the summer of 1944, when he surprised me by visiting me in New York, bringing me a copy of a piano version of Prokofiev's *Love for Three Oranges*. Always the teacher!

In 1980 Richter heard the name "Sophie Boekelheide" from Aberdeen, South Dakota, mentioned by Willard Scott on NBC's *Today Show* as one of his hundred-year-old honorees, Irving's aunt. She decided to try to find Irving, called an Aberdeen contact, and got his telephone number. But then: "I waited until 1995 to actually follow through when I really wanted to send him my latest CD [*Snow Mountain*] and let him know how much influence he had had on my personal and musical life, and that I actually had a career as a composer. I—finally called him. He was, of course, totally astounded."[10]

The two exchanged CDs of their music (Richter's was her *Snow Mountain* CD), and Richter was thrilled by his comments in a letter he wrote to her about her music:

> You certainly display a vivid, penetrating, fertile imagination, and the means of making a disciplined product with these enviable traits! I'm pleased to say that I feel, like you, similarities [between his music and hers]; in particular, the sense that this musical product itself describes, and circumscribes, subtle emotional euphoria, or mystique, or rapture, or fervency, and doesn't need to answer to anything else.[11]

The two soon lost touch again. He died in 2005.

The most important relationship from Richter's youth was with pianist Lenore Engdahl. In the summer of 1941, Richter won a scholarship to participate in piano master classes given in Minneapolis by the Polish pianist Countess Helena Morsztyn from New York. (Morsztyn had studied with Theodor Leschetizky, who had studied with Carl Czerny. Irene Hellner had studied with Morsztyn.) Here Richter met Morsztyn's prize student, Lenore Engdahl, age twenty-three at the time. A Minneapolis native, she studied with Morsztyn in New York but came home for the summer, partly to participate in these classes. Richter recalls:

> At the first class she played Bach's great *Fantasy and Fugue in G Minor* with such passion that I finally fell in love with Bach, and also experienced my third great attachment. I immediately sent her an unsigned letter expressing my great admiration for her playing and for herself. Then I brought myself to her attention at the next class by hovering about and staring at her, plainly awestruck, until she realized I was the letter writer. I admitted it, as was my intention, and she invited me to go out with her for ice cream. She went from being my idol and mentor, for whom I wrote my first eight extant pieces, to becoming a lifelong best friend and champion of my adult piano music.[12]

These works composed for Engdahl include five songs: *Jabberwocky* (Lewis Carroll), and *Four Songs*: "Alone" (Richter), "Midnight" (James Russell Lowell), "When I Am Not With You" (Sara Teasdale), and "Peace" (Richter); and three piano pieces: *Ballet of the Pixilated Penguins*, *March Berserk*, and *Dream Andante*.

Richter's continuing close feeling for Engdahl is shown in the dedications and playful nicknames she wrote on the title pages of the works:

> On *Jabberwocky*:
> To "General" Engdahl
> By "Lieutenant" Richter
>
> On "Alone":
> To Lenore: in memory of the day we met. June 30, 1941
> Lyrics and music by Lieutenant
>
> On "Midnight":
> Dedicated to "THE GENERAL" in commemoration
> of our First Anniversary
> By Lieutenant
>
> On "When I Am Not With You"
> Dedication: Censored. By order of General Kwasniewski
> Just a present for–Lenore-Feb. 6, 1944
>
> On "Peace"
> For Lenore: on our Third Anniversary—June 30th, 1944
> Inspired by my first Sunday Morning in Beechhurst
> By Marga Richter [she used "Florence Richter" prior to this]

On *March Berserk*
Written for my favorite pianist, Lenore Engdahl, with the hope that someday I may write something really worthy of her pianism.
April 8, 1945
By Marga Richter

On *Dream Andante*
In four years (to the day)
I've run out of things to say;
So I'll just put the date.
(You know how you rate.)
June 30, 1945.
By Marga Richter

The nicknames "Lieutenant" and "General" were prompted by the war going on at the time (World War II). "Kwasniewski" was Engdahl's husband, whom she later divorced.

During a long career of concertizing and teaching, Engdahl performed Richter's *Ballet of the Pixilated Penguins*, *Sonata for Piano*, and *Eight Pieces for Piano* on various occasions. In 2008 at the age of ninety, Lenore Engdahl remarked about Marga and her music:

> She isn't recognized the way she should be. And I don't know if it's because she's a woman or not. I've heard some contemporary musicians' music that I could hardly wait until it was over. But her music I find very engrossing. She sent me three little pieces,—I'm not up to learning a big piece. I did do her Sonata, and I played it in New York for a concert at Town Hall. And it's fabulous, it's a fabulous piece of music. But, it's so difficult to learn. First of all, because it's not the old European vi, V, IV chords, and so forth. It's very atonal and beautiful.
>
> One of the records I made for MGM was the Milhaud's *Saudades do Brasil*, and his music was my first introduction to something that wasn't all in harmony. And I loved it—the rhythms, absolutely fantastic music, and Marga's reminds me of that, but hers is more profound than the *Saudades do Brasil*. She has every emotion, every emotion, the gamut of emotion. These three pieces that I have . . . well, the *Pixilated Penguins* is just full of fun. Oh it's just full of the devil. And that's what she is like *[laughs]*. She's extremely serious, can be extremely serious, and profound, and yet she has this wonderful kind of humor. [She] picks it out of nowhere. I can't even explain to you. You've met her, so you know probably. . . . Very witty. And she does this in her music.[13]

Jabberwocky

Though *Jabberwocky* is Richter's earliest extant work, it contains all of the elements that she has used consistently throughout her life: chromaticism, free use of dissonance, rhythmic energy and clever rhythms, ostinato-based forms, and dramatic pacing. A repeated augmented octave (E♭–E) suggests the image of the "Jabberwock"; perfect fifths and perfect fourths, followed by minor ninths and minor seconds create dissonant, but recognizable patterns. The piece ends on a diminished octave (E–E♭). In some phrases, the singer can sing the melody doubled in the piano part; for others, the singer can simply speak the poem, sprechstimme-style, as the pianist plays evocative music.[14]

The first public performance of Richter's music came in 1941. She and her mother performed *Jabberwocky* at the Robbinsdale high school on a concert given by a choral group called the Mother Singers, directed by her mother. The two also performed *Midnight* on a recital at the MacPhail School of Music and later made a record of it. (She recalls the record being broken in 1942 when she slipped and fell with it on an icy step.)

New York City, 1943

In the summer of 1942, Morsztyn returned to Minneapolis, and Richter again attended her classes and also took private lessons to prepare for a solo recital at the MacPhail School. Richter's high school gave her six weeks' sabbatical from the fall term to do so. After the recital, Morsztyn suggested to her parents that she come to New York to study with her. Astonishingly, her parents agreed to this, and in 1943 Richter completed her senior year in a summer school session and the entire family moved to New York City.

Richter recalls:

> And the whole family (mother, father, brother, dog, plus my mother's Steinway upright piano) moved to New York—this was the extraordinary thing. Because they didn't think I should go alone. I think about that every little while, because to me it didn't seem so. . . . It seemed wonderful, but it didn't seem . . . why not? You know. And in fact . . . I think I lived all my life with blinders on, just thinking about the music and what I was doing and . . . I don't remember the conversation. . . . I do not remember my family coming to me and saying, "Would you like to go to New York?" or "We're going to New York." It was just . . . it became a fact. And we had to sell the house, and my father's business—he owned the local newspaper . . .[15]

It shows an extraordinary confidence in their daughter's talent for them to make such a move without really knowing where it might lead. They set up residence at 7 West 28th Street in Manhattan. Richter's father soon found employment selling life insurance, and her former-opera-star mother worked at the ribbon counter in a Woolworth store on 26th Street and Fifth Avenue to help defray expenses. Richter herself also needed to find a job to help out. In her words,

> My first interview was with the manager of a handbag factory in midtown Manhattan. He was right out of central casting, stocky, lecherous . . . I was, in effect, "just off the boat" innocent, timid, inexperienced, but when he put his hand on my knee and offered me the job (stock girl), even I knew enough to quickly decline, push his hand away, and rush out the door.[16]

She subsequently worked at a variety of jobs: in a slip (lingerie) factory, boxing orders; punching mailing lists into an addressograph machine; and delivering Western Union telegrams on foot in the 34th Street business area of Manhattan. After that she gradually built up a private piano practice.

Although still focusing on becoming a concert pianist, in February of 1944, Richter composed her *Ballet of the Pixilated Penguins* for piano solo and presented it to Engdahl, who was still living in New York. Engdahl gave the premiere on her October 22, 1944, recital at New York's Town Hall. She also played it at an audition for Leopold Stokowski (to play a concerto with his orchestra) when he asked if she could play a contemporary piece for him. It was the only one she had in her repertoire at that moment. As Engdahl reported to Richter, Stokowski became very excited about this piece by an unknown composer, and told Engdahl, "Tell her to never study composition formally. She will lose something very unique and fresh."[17] Despite not following his advice and soon entering the Juilliard School (called the Institute of Musical Arts until 1946),[18] Richter has always maintained her individuality and resisted systems of any sort.

The *Ballet of the Pixilated Penguins* reveals a playful side of Richter that she has maintained her whole life. She loves to use titles with double meanings, sign her works and dedicate them with special nicknames, and use musical elements (rests, syncopation, and chromaticism) to create humor and surprise in many of her compositions. With the signature "Pengy" on the original manuscript, the piece opens with an adulterated trumpetlike flourish in F minor. It has a syncopated ostinato in the left hand suggesting the quirky movements of the penguins, and a chromatically inflected right hand with pecking and sweeping melodic gestures. The figuration includes repeated chromatic triplets, chromatic scales in each hand, a half-step apart, and some sixteenth-note passages with both hands in octaves. (In 2005 she used this piece, with minor alterations, in her *Divers (Diverse) Divertimento* for flute, oboe, and guitar.)

In the spring of 1944, Richter gave her first New York piano recital at the Studio Club. She decided that this was a good time to begin using her middle name, Marga, rather than her first name. She had always felt that "Florence" sounded too "goody-goody" and straight-laced. With this name change, she feels, a freer personality emerged.

The Juilliard Years: 1945–51

In 1945, after her second Studio Club recital, Richter's parents decided it would be beneficial for her to change teachers again and receive the broader musical education available at Juilliard. She applied and was accepted as a piano major under Rosalyn Tureck. Richter reflected on her studies with Tureck:

> What she taught me about rhythm was a revelation. She stressed the importance of lightly accenting the first beat of the metrical unit and creating tension in a phrase by understanding and projecting the rhythmic structure. In addition we were taught to incorporate an infinitesimal pause between the beats (the "agogic accent") which creates great rhythmic excitement and interest. This was revelatory to me and is totally responsible for what I consider one of the most important aspects of the structure and impact of my music.[19]

Also in 1945, while attending the Juilliard summer session theory classes, Richter met Eliot Philips, trombonist, who became her first real boyfriend. Their intense relationship was short-lived, but a lasting legacy was his influence in convincing her to be politically liberal. Accordingly, in 1948 she voted for Democrat Harry Truman. (Her father had been an anti-Roosevelt Republican, but later switched parties and backed Adlai Stevenson and campaigned for Hubert Humphrey.) Richter, Philips, and his wife Sylvia have remained friends throughout the years. "I mate for life," she jokes.

At the end of Richter's first year, Tureck resigned from Juilliard to devote her career to concertizing. However, she offered to continue teaching two students privately, and Richter was one of them. Richter was delighted that she could continue studying with Tureck but needed to find a new major in order to remain at the school. She cavalierly applied as a composer and was accepted. She said:

> The compositions I submitted with my application were not very good, and I doubt they would meet today's standards. Perhaps I was accepted because they could see I was not just a casual songwriter. It might have been because they thought they could make something of me![20]

Richter studied with William Bergsma for one year (1946–47), after which Bergsma took a short leave from Juilliard. (He later returned and became associate dean.) Richter laughs as she recalls an interviewer joking with her in 1976, "when Marga Richter entered the Juilliard School, the faculty fled." About Bergsma, Richter says:

> William Bergsma made me feel like a composer, but he wasn't specific about stuff. He would just get excited about everything. And we actually had group lessons. I think there were two or three of us at once. And we went through music and we tried to write stuff. The stuff I wrote that year was pretty much terrible.[21]

In the fall of 1947, Richter began studies with a new professor, Vincent Persichetti, with whom she studied for the remainder of her time at Juilliard.[22] About Persichetti, Richter says:

> Persichetti was a very good teacher. I think he's the person who encouraged my natural bent to have the music *arrive* somewhere. He was very big on having it go someplace. Make some sense out of it. The only thing he didn't do was teach me anything about orchestration. Which is surprising, because he was so good at that. I had to learn that later, way later.[23]

In an interview with Jane LePage, Richter said about both Bergsma and Persichetti, "Unlike so many composition teachers, they did not try to turn me into weak carbon copies of themselves but helped me learn how to make my own musical ideas into finished pieces."[24]

Persichetti's own compositional style relied on much counterpoint that exploited modern musical vocabulary from diatonicism to atonality, self-borrowings, counterpoint, great stylistic freedom, and short sections based on single themes building into larger structures. Many of his compositions were for band instruments, piano, or for children. Highly regarded as a teacher, Persichetti both started and ended his 1961 *Twentieth-Century Harmony* text with the following lines expressing his attitude toward composition:

> Any tone can succeed any other tone, any tone can sound simultaneously with any other tone or tones, and any group of tones can be followed by any other group of tones, just as any degree of tension or nuance can occur in any medium under any kind of stress or duration. Successful projection will depend upon the contextual and formal conditions that prevail, and upon the skill and the soul of the composer.[25]

In addition to her teachers, Richter has cited the works of Machaut, J. S. Bach, Beethoven, Bartók, Hovhaness, Shostakovich, and Stravinsky as being inspirational during her time at Juilliard.

> I like the rhythmic and harmonic strength in Bach, and perhaps the formal architecture of Beethoven. And I have to admit I especially like Bartók and Shostakovich. Shostakovich, I just love it. The sound of minor sevenths and ninths that I heard from Shostakovich's works was a theme I had been using a lot. The same notes, but a different rhythm. Bartók—I like his rhythms, especially *Music for Strings, Percussion, and Celesta* (1936) and *Mikrokosmos* (1926–37). I also like Hovhaness's modal and oriental harmony, especially in his *St. Vartan Symphony* (1951). I admire Stravinsky's rhythmic divisions and metrical displacement in *Symphony of Psalms* (1930).[26]

In March 1948, while studying at the Juilliard School, Richter composed her exhilarating three-movement *Sonata for Clarinet and Piano*. It was premiered there by clarinetist Herbert Tichman with Richter at the piano on November 11, 1948. Richter recalls that audience reactions ranged from composer Wallingford Riegger's "There's genius here," to Suzanne Bloch's "It's frightening to think of one so young writing a piece like this!" Emboldened by such responses, Richter took the work to a leading publisher, who commented cryptically "an extraordinary composition for a young lady" and declined to publish it.[27]

The piece, which has no key signature, is rhythmically exciting with its constant metric changes, and uses articulation as an important structural element. In the first movement, motives in the clarinet are continuously transformed. At the climax the pianist plays barrages of chords in triplet rhythms alternating between the hands, or vigorous octaves in both hands that expand from the center of the piano outward. At the end of the first movement, the intensity subsides and the music proceeds attacca into the more romantic second movement. It begins slowly, mournfully, in the Phrygian mode, and features long winding melodic lines with a steady quarter-note pulse. Eventually the pace quickens, the calm is shattered, and each instrument has a short but wild cadenza before a return of the opening material, now compressed into a quasi coda. The final spirited movement has a driving motoric rhythm, again with constantly changing meters, and Richter's characteristic dissonances of seconds, sevenths, and diminished octaves.

About her *Sonata for Clarinet and Piano*, Richter says,

> it's an incredible piece for [the age when I wrote it]—I don't know, it just came out of nowhere. Up until then I had written . . . stuff . . . then suddenly I wrote this piece and it was . . . like a shorter practice piece for the *Sonata for Piano* . . . it was sort of the same kind of form and everything. I found . . . my rhythmic excitement, and harmony, everything. And I just started pouring it out, I didn't think about it.[28]

Subsequent performers of the sonata have included clarinetists Joseph Rutkowski, Naomi Drucker, and Donald Gephardt, all with Richter; clarinetist Mariko Sudo, with pianist Maria Salabasheva, included it in her master's-degree recital at the Manhattan School of Music on January 29, 2006.

Beginning in 1948, a series of upheavals occurred in Richter's life. In March of 1948 Richter's mother and brother moved back to Minneapolis so that he could attend the University of Minnesota. Her father joined them a few weeks later after making sure Richter had found a renter for a room in the apartment. As it turned out, Rosalyn Tureck arranged for her sister Margaret to be that person. After she moved in they became "buddies" (Margaret even taught Richter to make cabbage and beet borscht) and had long talks about love and life and politics, including the impending creation of the state of Israel. Richter recalls: "On Israeli Independence Day, May 14, we were both ecstatically jumping up and down and screaming!"[29]

In May 1948, Richter met physicist Vernon Hughes (1921–2003) who was working on his doctorate at Columbia University. Less than four months later they married, on August 13, a Friday. (Richter jokes that it may have been a poor idea to tempt fate.)

She describes selecting the wedding venue:

> After we had decided to be married in Massachusetts, we needed to find a church. Our method was to find a general location, get onto a local-area bus and get off when we saw a pretty church. We found the perfect church in Annisquam, then located the pastor and asked if he would marry us. He agreed and asked why we had picked this area. I gave what I thought was a perfectly reasonable answer; "His mother lives in New York and my family lives in Minnesota, so we decided to get married here."[30]

Her choice of wedding dress was also unconventional. It was a navy-blue lace three-quarter-length strapless gown that she selected because it could later be used for concertizing. (She wore it when she and Herbert Tichman premiered her *Sonata for Clarinet and Piano* in the Juilliard concert hall that November.)

Margaret Tureck eventually moved out of the apartment, and the newlyweds had the place to themselves until early in 1949, when Hughes's mother moved in. Marga describes this: "This was not a harmonious situation. The friction between us was palpable. When I overheard Vernon's defense of me to his mother ('Marga's not so bad') the seeds for eventual dissolution of the marriage were sown. On the night in question, I quietly left the apartment without a word and spent the night with a friend, leaving Vernon clueless and worried. We patched things up when I returned in the morning."[31]

In the fall of 1949 the three moved to a larger apartment on 118th Street near Columbia University, where Hughes was pursuing his postdoctorate. The strained relationship between the two women intensified, and early in 1950 Richter moved out, to a rooming house on 122nd Street and Amsterdam, a block from Juilliard, taking her Baldwin grand piano with her. Soon, Hughes asked his mother to move out, and Richter and her piano moved back in.

During this stressful time, Richter went to a Reichian therapist. Reichian therapy involved relieving tension through deep-tissue massage, dream analysis, and uninhibited vocal reaction to emotional insights (often this was screaming). The therapist would usually start by focusing on the eyes and on respiration. Richter remembers Persichetti commenting soon after she began the therapy that the little lines around her eyes were gone. Another supposed benefit of the therapy is increased sexual freedom and satisfaction.

In Richter's case this therapy allowed her to accept her growing emotional involvement with a fellow Juilliard composer. She recollects that he had become infatuated with her upon hearing the recording of her clarinet sonata in the Juilliard library and then meeting her at the weekly gathering of a small group of Juilliard composition students (all male) at a local bar. (This is where she began to enjoy a convivial glass of beer along with the attention of many of these colleagues. She recalls that they sometimes argued as to who would walk her home). As this clandestine relationship deepened, it became clear to her that her marriage was no longer viable.

Richter recounts that, disregarding her therapist's advice to not leave her husband only because of feelings for another man, she went home after a particularly insightful and emotional session, locked herself in the bathroom, had a cathartic crying episode, emerged at Hughes's urging and told him she wanted a divorce. According to Richter, he pleaded with her, but she would not be dissuaded. An additional reason for leaving this marriage was Hughes's recent statement that their lives were perhaps too busy to allow for the disruption of having a family. As Richter, and her piano, moved out for good, she left her diamond-studded wedding band and a note on the hall table.[32]

In 1950, the State of New York did not have no-fault divorce, so Richter went to Jacksonville, Florida, in April to establish (fake) residency and returned three months later to receive the decree, dated July 24, 1950.

In spite of this personal turmoil, during the spring of 1949 she composed her song cycle *Transmutation*, still performed, and an orchestra piece (which is lost, and unlamented by Richter) to satisfy the requirements for her bachelor's degree of that year.

Transmutation is a setting of eight texts by various Chinese poets, translated by Henry H. Hart: "Twilight" (Ch'en Yün), "The Orchid" (Liu Sung), "Change" (Hsaio Kang), "Desolation" (Chang Chi), "On Seeing a Red Cockatoo on the Road to Mount Shang" (Po Chü I), "Sleeplessness" (Anonymous), "A Song of Ch'ang An" (Anonymous), and "Transmutation" (Anonymous). In this work, Richter is sensitive to the symbolic meanings in the texts and captures the mood of the poetry exquisitely using sparse textures and harmonies. Her interest in Chinese poetry would continue in 1953, when she composed two more songs, "The Hermit" and "Fishing Picture" (see chapter 2).

Richter opted to take off the 1949–50 academic year before enrolling in the master's degree program at Juilliard, but she was allowed to continue her lessons with Persichetti and attend the weekly composition forums. The composer Irwin Bazelon attended as a guest one day early in 1950 to ask if anyone would volunteer to perform his Piano Sonata No. 2 at an International Society for Contemporary Music (ISCM) concert in April. Because of the turmoil in her private life and the fact that she had time on her hands due to her curtailed Juilliard schedule (although she had a large class of private piano students), she immediately raised her hand. (She feels that this was the single most important gesture of her life.) The concert took place on April 9, 1950, in New York, after she had left Hughes. She recalls that her page turner was the man she left him for and that the full-blown romance peaked, then soon subsided and ended, which briefly broke her heart.[33]

However, the connection with Bazelon endured. He became her unofficial promoter and arranged an "audition" with the director of the Composers Forum in New York, a prestigious new music series. The director listened to her clarinet sonata and was overwhelmed with its originality, surprised it was written by a woman, especially one so young. He immediately booked her for the coming season.[34]

After Richter had moved to New York, she had befriended Phyllis Latimer.[35] Latimer lived with the Richter family briefly at West 28th Street while studying composition herself at the Juilliard Graduate School. Latimer liked to use Richter's piano at that time. Latimer, who is just a few years older than Richter, continued to compose now and then, and went on to have a career as a painter and poet. The two have remained in touch to this day, and Richter visited Latimer in 1996 in Seattle when Richter's *Out of Shadows and Solitude* was recorded.

Latimer recalls their "mutual love of quirky, creative things to do together." She recalls seeing a very tall building in silhouette on the top of the New Jersey ridge across the Hudson and spontaneously deciding together to walk to it! "This involved walking many blocks south to find a ferry, then walking north and west on the other side till we found it." She also remembers "Both of us were working on the Bach two-part inventions, so we decided we would sing them while on the back seat of the city bus on the way to Juilliard. It was a challenge because the range went all over, and we had to switch octaves as needed. And it was fun, both to sing them, and to enjoy heads turning as people wanted to see what was going on back there."[36]

In 1950, Richter composed *Into What Unknown Chamber* for voice and piano, a setting of three brief poems by Latimer, "A Butterfly," "Tense Day," and "Shadows of Dead Flowers." They are freely dissonant works, without key signatures, that are rhythmically sensitive to the texts. The last one is marked "In strict time; vocal line more spoken than sung—emphasis on consonants" at the beginning and "sing normally" at the end.

While *Into What Unknown Chamber* is a minor one in her output, Richter's initial friendship with Latimer ushered in a period of expanded horizons, of experimenting with different ways of living one's life with more freedom and fewer boundaries. Latimer is a Theosophist and in the summer of 1950 she invited Richter to join her at a Theosophical camp, Camp Indralaya, on Orcas Island in the San Juan Islands of Washington State. This was right after Richter's divorce had come through. She took a bus from Jacksonville, Florida, where she had gone to finalize her divorce, to Seattle, and on to the camp.

Richter attended the camp for two summers, in 1950 and 1951, experimenting with different ways of living life with more freedom and fewer boundaries. Looking back, Richter felt that she had been somewhat repressed until that time. Here she lived close to nature, getting water from a pump, sleeping in a cabin or outside under the stars, taking showers with water buckets in an open-to-the-sky wooden enclosure, and eating only vegetarian food. She attended nightly campfire gatherings where there were philosophical lectures and discussions and musical entertainment in which she participated, playing Bartók on an old upright piano. She stopped curling her hair and enjoyed walks in the rain, feeling more free and natural. (Richter later joked that she liked the Bohemian lifestyle long before the "hippies" came along.)

In the fall of 1950, Richter resumed her studies at Juilliard, now in the master's degree program in composition. And, on February 3, 1951, the aforementioned Composers Forum concert took place at the McMillan Theatre at Columbia University.[37] Four works from Richter's Juilliard years were performed: *Sonata for Clarinet and Piano* (Herbert Tichman, clarinet; Marga Richter, piano), *Transmutation* and *Into What Unknown Chamber* (Phyllis Goodmund, soprano, Marga Richter piano), and *String Quartet No. 1*. The concerts received positive reviews from both the *New York Herald Tribune* and the *New York Times*.

> Miss Richter's evolution should be allowed to follow its own inner nature, avoiding formula or systems as much as possible. The most valuable of her musical attributes are an original sense of rhythm, a sense of drama in choice of materials and, above all, an ability to make her own forms grow from the very nature of her materials and ideas. This is the very essence of composition and to let any "system" obscure its development would be a great pity.[38]

> Miss Richter's works were restless, inventive, dissonant, clean, and her intentions seemed to be well-realized. [The string quartet] . . . gave one the impression that he had experienced something real. . . . We will hear more from Miss Richter.[39]

These positive reviews were, of course, extremely encouraging to the young composer.

At the time, serialism and an emphasis on precompositional planning and complex structures were the dominant trends in composition. In 2005 Richter reflected on the prevailing practices:

> It was just awful because I was trying to do it by making up some rhythms and form . . . I was trying to do what people were telling you to do, what you had to do to write a piece, you had to plan it all out—it was terrible.[40]

Richter's further comments on the first *String Quartet* reveal her disdain for the twelve-tone system:

> [The first String Quartet is] . . . not viable. I have it, but it's not playable. The second movement has something that I took and used for my piano sonata. You know—Don't throw anything away, there might be one little nugget there that you can use. And the opening theme was actually a twelve-tone theme. It's kind of cute—you wouldn't know it was twelve-tone . . . I tried to do that, but . . . and you know, at that time, boy, if you wrote a triad, you were like "blaagh." You know *[laughs]*. So I did it anyway. *Lament* is pretty . . . it's not conventional, but it's emotional. And that was written in 1956, when everybody had to write the most disjunct, abstract, dissonant stuff. So they turned their noses up. Then when *they* started doing it, when George Rochberg saw the light, and John Corigliano came along, well, they were heroes because they dared to do this, and my piece did it twenty years earlier, but at that time you were scoffed at, so this whole thing just makes me sort of . . . sick.[41]

When asked if she thought serialism was in some way a "masculine" style, Richter gave a response that shows her rejection of overly attended-to formal concerns:

> Yes, probably. Because men just like to have form over content. *[Laughs]* I mean, look . . . Most of the great composers were men. The ones we know about. So, men were . . . They were great—I love them. But uh . . . twelve-tone music—does it make any sense to you? Why bother? Especially when you get to the point where you say, "well, let's mitigate this a little. Let's get the sharp edges off. You can repeat a note once, but not twice . . ." Why not just write something from your heart? . . . It's not my cup of tea . . . or coffee.[42]

Despite this perspective, Richter did experiment once in 1952 with her own precompositional systematic approach that she used in her *7E* for wind quintet. She later dismissed this as well, describing it as "stupid, based on an invented system of sevenths."[43]

In addition to the works on the Composers Forum concert, Richter had composed two other, subsequently withdrawn, works during her Juilliard years: *All Desire Is Sad* (1950), a modern dance score, choreographed by Katherine Litz, for a collaboration between the Juilliard School's music and dance departments; and *Relations* (1951), a cantata with text by Gerd Stern for mixed chorus and small orchestra.

All Desire Is Sad, scored for chamber orchestra, was performed in the Juilliard Concert Hall in February 1951. This was Richter's first dance score. When Litz subsequently presented this work at the YMHA (Young Men's Hebrew Association at Lexington Ave. and 92nd Street), which Richter attended, an announcement was made to the audience, just before intermission, that music by Duke Ellington would be substituted for one section to replace Richter's faux-jazzy dance sequence in $\frac{5}{4}$, featuring syncopation and prominent double-bass pizzicati. Richter was incensed and briefly considered striding to the stage and demanding the performance be canceled, as she imagined Beethoven doing, but she was too timid to do so. When she wrote to Litz about this substitution, Litz replied, "I never liked your music for this section." (Twenty years later, Richter did have the courage to change her music and the choreography of the ballet score to *Abyss*, during intermission. But this time it was her own decision. See chapter 3.) Although not viable as a concert piece, Richter salvaged the faux-jazz section as prime material for a 1991 orchestral work, *Quantum Quirks of a Quick Quaint Quark*.

Richter had met Gerd Stern in the fall of 1950. They became friends, and early in 1951 she decided to collaborate with him on *Relations*, for submission as her composition project for her master's degree. The text was extremely esoteric, which appealed to her because it was philosophically challenging. The music is disjunct, dissonant, and succinct, in keeping with the terse poetry. The committee was suitably impressed, and she received her degree.

Through the efforts of Stern, who brought the score to the attention of conductor Leon Barzin, the cantata was given a rehearsal reading by the National Orchestral Association on March 25, 1951. It was broadcast on WNYC in New York. Richter was in the studio to converse with Barzin, answer questions, and supply commentary. Margaret Hillis prepared the chorus. Stern, unable to attend, listened to the broadcast. In 2009 Stern and Richter reconnected, had the old 78s transferred to a CD, and listened to it together. She remained resigned that this music was not viable and joked, "The verdict was that perhaps a premiere at this late date might be feasible, but would it be wise?"[44]

When Richter graduated in 1951 from the Juilliard School of Music with a master's degree in composition, she was the first female to do so. At the time, the master's was the highest degree offered in composition. (In 1975 Ellen Taaffe Zwilich became the first female composer to receive a doctorate from Juilliard.)

The summer after her graduation, Richter returned to Camp Indralaya and this time worked part-time as a kitchen helper to defray expenses. She made friends with a professional pianist and her scientist husband who were living an alternative lifestyle on Orcas Island. In addition to being vegetarians, the couple consumed copious amounts of all-natural vitamins; banished all fats except natural oils; drank a concoction of brewer's yeast, blackstrap molasses, and raw milk; used herbal tea in place of coffee; and never touched alcohol. Richter attributes her continuing good health to incorporating some of these practices into her own life, though she does drink alcohol.[45]

The three of them bonded immediately, and she was invited to stay with them for a month after the camp session ended, becoming a "second wife." Richter recalls:

> This is when my life became very interesting. I became part of their family. Their two young sons called me their second mommy. I adopted their weird sleeping regimen which was to sleep two hours, do creative work for two hours, return to sleep for two hours, etc.; I really was able to memorize Bach fugues, for instance, quite easily. My mental functions were enhanced with extraordinary clarity. The closeness that developed among us was so strong that it was suggested I become a permanent part of the family when they left the island and returned to their professional teaching commitments. When I demurred because I wanted to have my own children and would thus need my own husband (this was in the time when "nice" women did not have children on their own), we briefly considered having the two of them divorce, he would marry me, I would have a child and then they would remarry. We soon abandoned this convoluted scenario. They went back to their "real" life, and I went back to New York. But I was now a much freer person, open to passionate adventures in life and new paths in creating music.[46]

This was the second time Richter backed away from a man in part because of her desire to have children.

Despite some personal turmoil with her early marriage and divorce, Richter had experienced a significant amount of success and was eager to see what the future would hold.

2 Modern Dance and the MGM Recordings *1951–1960*

The greatest satisfaction—it sounds kind of dumb to say this—is writing the music. There is nothing as exciting as knowing that you've written something that you really love.

Marga Richter, interview by André Bernard, 1985

AFTER HER GRADUATION from Juilliard, Richter moved to 308 West 107th Street, where she enjoyed having her first apartment all to herself. Living in New York City with its myriad of artistic opportunities was a great advantage for a composer, and she was able to attend fine traditional and new music concerts, visit museums, and partake in the cultural life of the city. However, earning a living was a significant concern for Richter, and she reflected on her own initial uncertainty after graduation.

> I suddenly said, "Well here I am, I have my master's degree. I don't know what to do with myself. What do I do now?" You know, I have a feeling that if you were a male composer, somebody told you what to do, "go to Tanglewood, do this, do that, do something." But they expected women composers were just going to go off and get married, do nothing, and they didn't have to bother with us.[1]

Perhaps Richter was not groomed for success to the same degree as her male counterparts. Among Richter's good friends at Juilliard were composers Jacob Druckman (1928–1996), Hall Overton (1920–1972), and Hugh Aitken (b. 1924). Like Richter, all three studied composition with Vincent Persichetti. They each went on to achieve significant public success as composers, and all three taught for some time at Juilliard. Druckman was able to continue his studies with a Fulbright

Fellowship at the École Normale de Musique in Paris and won the Pulitzer Prize for composition in 1972. Richter, on the other hand, was "on her own."

Modern Dance

Fortunately, Richter's music had drawn the attention of choreographer James Waring, who had attended her Composers Forum concert. Upon her return from Orcas Island in September, she received a postcard from him saying he liked her music very much and asking if she would like to compose a score for him. She readily agreed, without so much as meeting him first. Because the best time for him was 10 P.M., after his shift in the Time Inc. mail room, and his apartment was in Hell's Kitchen in Manhattan, where he lived with the dancer and choreographer Alec Rubin, he arranged to meet her in a church in the area and escort her to his home. Richter recalled:

> I wasn't at all afraid of going to his apartment with him. I was too innocent to think that something would . . . I mean you just don't think in those terms, not then, and maybe never; if somebody wants to work with you, you go to their house, you don't think about it.[2]

Richter's reflection on this meeting shows that she was independent, trusting, and focused on her work.

A short time after she agreed to work with Waring, Gerd Stern invited her to visit him in New Paltz, New York, where he was living in a small farmhouse as an all-purpose handyman for the owner, Thorberg Ellison. Stern was interested in persuading creative people to come to live there in a communal atmosphere. Ellison was interested in generating income by renting rooms in her house or in the spacious three-unit chicken house. Richter recalls:

> I went there for a weekend, was captivated by the idea and immediately agreed to rent one of the units, for an astonishing $60 a year! I also enthusiastically agreed to devote two weekends, prior to moving in, to sweeping out the chicken detritus (from a 30-by-15-foot main room) and pouring insulation between inner and outer walls, wearing a mask. Sometime after I moved in I was also assigned the task of tarring the roof. Being afraid of heights, this required more courage than I knew I had, which delighted me. But negotiating getting back onto the ladder to descend was too scary and I had to call, loudly and repeatedly, for help.[3]

After Richter moved, she arranged to spend three days each week in New York to teach her piano students and meet with Waring as she worked on her dance score, *The Wanderers* (1952). Since he did not have a piano, they met at the apartment of his friends, Edward Cole, director of classical music for Metro-Goldwyn-Mayer Records (MGM), and Alan Skelly (1921–1988), who offered the use of his piano and an old guitar. (Richter recalls using the guitar to pluck out a theme used in *The Wanderers* and years later in her second string quartet.) At the time, Skelly, a Harvard graduate in English, worked for Time Inc., where James Waring was also employed.

The routine of traveling back and forth from New Paltz to Manhattan ended abruptly on Saturday, January 14, 1952, when a fire burned the entire chicken house to the ground, and, along with it, Richter's 6′3″ Baldwin grand piano and all of her music. Fortunately, copies of her own music were preserved in other places. Richter received the news early on Sunday morning, having overnighted at the home of Elizabeth (Betty) Olsen, a pianist friend from Juilliard.[4] Richter remarks:

> The knowledge that I now owned nothing but the clothes I had with me and a pair of ice skates (Betty and I had been to the Central Park rink) was devastating at the time but oddly freeing later on. I arrived in New Paltz at 3 A.M. Monday, viewed the eerie scene of the remnants of my possessions strewn about on the snow-covered hills and went into the farmhouse to sleep in a room devoid of heat, because Ellison blamed me for the fire and thought I would start another one. Perhaps as a result of this environment, plus the stress of starting over, I became ill and moved back to Manhattan into a rooming house. Here I developed full-blown pneumonia, begged help from one of my adult students, Lenore Schneiderman, who took me into her own home and called a doctor. Fearing I might die, the doctor asked whom they should notify. Schneiderman did not know. Fortunately, I did not die, and while I was recovering, the insurance adjuster came by and, perhaps touched by my condition, granted the full amount of my claim.[5]

With a portion of the insurance money, Richter was able to purchase the hand-decorated hundred-year-old Steinway-grand converted player-piano that she has to this day.

After she recovered, Richter moved into composer Elizabeth (Betty) Sawyer's Greenwich Village apartment at 78 Bedford Street, about eight blocks away from Alan Skelly's apartment, where she attended the frequent meetings of Dance Associates, a group of choreographers, dancers, and composers cofounded by Waring and Rubin. In these social gatherings her relationship with Skelly blossomed.

During this upheaval, Richter was unable to complete the Waring score in time for the premiere, so a colleague, Rudy Crosswell, wrote one short section, successfully imitating her style, and the performance took place on March 29, 1952, at the YMHA in Manhattan. Richter laughed when she remembered the performance:

> It was not good. The eight instrumentalists rehearsed only once, just before the performance, and without the dancers, who worked only with piano. . . . The bassoon player in particular was really bad, and in the middle of the performance he managed to pull the light cord out of the wall by mistake . . . the conductor and the instrumentalists couldn't see anything for several seconds. *That* helped![6]

5. *Alan Skelly, 1950s.*

Richter then composed a larger work, *Johnny Got His Gun*, based on the book of the same title by Dalton Trumbo. The choreographer was Irving Burton.[7] Scored for chamber orchestra, this work was presented on January 25, 1953, also at the YMHA. It is a dark story about a U.S. soldier who loses his arms, legs, eyes, ears, mouth, and nose. Richter has characterized the music as "sort of my Aaron Copland moment—the tunes were very prairielike. I don't think it was orchestrated very well, but it was effectively presented."[8] Richter reused themes from this work later in her *String Quartet No. 2* and in her *Variations on a Theme by Latimer* for piano four-hands.

Richter's third dance score, *The Vagabonds*, was choreographed by Alec Rubin.[9] This lighthearted work for two pianos and percussion tells the story of a ragtag group fleeing a villain and building a spaceship to flee from him. It was presented at the YMHA in May 1953 with Richter and Sawyer as the pianists. This score later evolved into Richter's *Melodrama* for two pianos without the percussion.

These works gave Richter valuable experience connecting music with motion, generating material, and strengthening her professional identity. She remarked in 2005 about these works, "The reason they're interesting is because I stole from them to use in later pieces. They're source materials."[10]

Second Marriage and Family

During this time Richter became increasingly close to Alan Skelly, and in 1953, they were married. Though she legally changed her last name to "Skelly," she kept "Marga Richter" as her professional name and always signs her works this way.

After their marriage, the couple moved to 875 West End Avenue at 103rd Street in Manhattan, where they lived for five years. Skelly was a good match for Richter, as he was interested in the creative process and the arts in general in addition to fundamental questions about the nature of the universe. He introduced Richter to astrology when they first met, and over time he became increasingly interested in Buddhism. Skelly later earned a Master of Arts in philosophy at the New School and eventually became chair of the Philosophy Department at C. W. Post College on Long Island.

Richter's musical work was fascinating to Skelly, who was a great appreciator of music. He was an amateur violinist, had sung in a choir at Harvard, and had even composed two little piano pieces that would be recorded by Richter for MGM Records and published by Leeds Music. (Skelly humorously remarked that he was the only U.S. composer whose complete output was published and recorded.) He was also at one point the president of the Huntington Symphony Association. Throughout their marriage Skelly placed a great priority on Richter's career. He admired and respected her music and often acted as something of an agent, helping in numerous ways to promote her works. Skelly also had an extensive knowledge of poetry and literature and would occasionally suggest texts to her. His Irish heritage in particular (his mother emigrated from Ireland and although he was born in the United States, he called himself fifteen sixteenths Irish) strongly influenced his bringing Irish and English sources to her attention.

In 1954, there was a production of Kurt Weill's *The Three-Penny Opera* at the off-Broadway Theatre de Lys (in New York), starring the renowned Lotte Lenya, his widow. Richter, Skelly, and Cole attended the premiere, after which Cole arranged to record a cast album of the work for MGM.[11] Richter attended the recording sessions as Cole's consultant and became friendly with Lenya, who had married U.S. writer and editor George Davis. Lenya invited Richter, Cole, and Skelly to spend the summer at their home in New City, New York, so that Skelly and Cole could sort and catalog great piles of Weill's music, left in chaos after his death.[12] She had been unable to find anyone she could trust to do this. They accepted, commuted to their work in New York City, and spent evenings and weekends on the Weill project. On commission from MGM, Richter spent her days working on an instrumental suite derived from Weill's opera *Mahagonny*. One afternoon toward the middle of August, Richter, in her first pregnancy, suffered a miscarriage. No one was there to care for her except George Davis, and "he rose to the occasion compassionately and competently," Richter recalls. Skelly returned soon and took her to a New York hospital. The *Mahagonny Suite* was never recorded.

6. Marga Richter in recording studio, 1954. From left to right: stage director Carmen Capalbo, musical director Samuel Matlowsky?, composer Marc Blitzstein, Marga Richter (seated), Lotte Lenya, and record producer Edward Cole. Photo by Jerry Saltsberg and Associates.

Richter and Skelly soon did have two children, a son Michael in 1955, and a daughter Maureen in 1957. (Richter recalls Lenya visiting her in the hospital when Michael was born.) In 1958, the family moved to a home on Long Island, where the children grew up and Richter continued to live until 2009.[13]

From 1956 to 1971, in keeping with the times, Richter became the primary day-to-day caregiver for the children as she continued composing, albeit less than before, and teaching piano privately; Skelly's career provided financial security. Richter describes working while the children were in school. She has said: "I'm glad, I think, that I didn't have commissions coming in and deadlines to meet while the kids were growing up. To tell them, go away I'm busy—I don't think I could have done this. Your kids are only home once, even if you live to be a hundred."[14]

In 2005 she reflected back on her career, "If I hadn't stopped to have children.

. . . Maybe some of the women composers who have done better don't have any kids, so they could go all out. All that energy that we put into being mothers, which I wouldn't trade for anything, takes your life for a long time."[15]

Not only was Richter involved with her own children, but she loves children in general. She is often fascinated by their unique interactions with people and their environment. Like a child herself in some ways, she laughs easily, which may seem unexpected for one who writes such serious music. She is definitely connected emotionally to the people around her.

Although Richter never taught composition, she did inspire some younger composers, including Dianne Goolkasian Rahbee, who babysat for her while a student at Juilliard. Rahbee's recollection addresses motherhood, working as a composer, and music:

> Marga was an inspiration and wonderful role-model for me. She was a woman composer of great accomplishment, a devoted wife and mother, and was able to manage it all! This is no easy feat, as I later found out in my own life. I would arrive at her apartment at 8:00 A.M. or earlier daily and baby sit for three or four hours while she was in the music room composing. I remember her working on only one measure sometimes for the entire three hours! She would endlessly repeat chords and phrases, each time making various modifications until she was completely satisfied with the results. It was really hard work and very intense. Sometimes when I babysat in the evening when the children were sleeping, I listened to some of her records, but was astonished when I found so few. She had almost exclusively Bach and the Beethoven String Quartets. When I asked her if she had more recordings, she said "What else do I need?!" I always remembered that statement. She studied piano at Juilliard with Rosalyn Tureck, the great Bach scholar. For my birthday, she also gave me a recording of the Swingle Singers singing various keyboard music of Bach. I was surprised at her flexibility in accepting this arrangement of Bach's music. It opened my mind to new and more free ways of thinking about music.[16]

An important factor in Richter successfully managing both a professional career and a traditional woman's role was the wholehearted support she received from her husband and her children. She recalls:

> As far as Alan is concerned, I think the whole thing of having a husband who provides an atmosphere where your music is more important than whether you cook a meal [was the key]. He'd often say jokingly, 'why are you cleaning? Go in there and write a symphony!' And the children also had that feeling. . . . My son when he was about twelve years old was helping me by putting in bar lines 'cause I had to do this thing [*Bird of Yearning*] in a big hurry. He didn't actually copy the music, but he was in on it.[17]

Richter has also described coordinating the various roles that many women find challenging.

> I had a studio out in the garage for a long time, and the children would come home from school. . . . Anytime they would knock on the door, I would always talk to them. But they also knew that I wanted to be private; it wasn't a matter of shutting them out. Summer vacations I used to put the music away and we went on trips. And we took a seven-week trip out west and stuff like that. We took the whole summer, and I was just a mother. The minute they got on the school bus, I was a composer. So I was lucky to have people around me that understood all that.[18]

Her daughter Maureen's remarks show the strong bonds she has with her children:

> We always came first in her life. She knows what's important. I love to be around her because she takes such joy in everything in life. . . . She just had great wisdom in balancing her life. She had good priorities. She just understood that 'I'm a mother and I have to do that. And yet I'm also a composer and I have to do that.' [Giving up composition] would be like giving up breathing; for her it's the driving force of her existence. She just believes in the music. She knows it's good and she knows it's worthwhile. She knows her music moves people and that's of great value to her.[19]

In a separate anecdote, in regard to her writing *Landscapes of the Mind I* (1968–74), Richter laughed as she recalled Michael asking:

> "How many measures did you write today?" and I said "Five" and he said "And how many did you take out?" And I said, "Three" *[laughs]*. He knew how fussy I was and how hard this piece was to get right . . . he was fourteen at the time and asked, "Are you writing for fame and money or the art form?" "I'm writing for fame and money," I said. And he said, "well I think you'd better write a little faster!"[20]

While Richter does mention fame and money here in a humorous conversation, it is clear that she was most interested in expressing emotion and creating beauty with her music.

MGM Recordings

From 1953 to 1957, following her work with the Dance Associates and her marriage, Richter composed a rich variety of concert music commissioned by Edward Cole for recording by MGM: *Sonata for Piano* (1954), *Concerto for Piano and Violas, Cellos and Basses* (1955) (also called *Piano Concerto No. 1*), *Lament* for string orchestra (1956), and *Aria and Toccata* for viola and string orchestra (1957). In addition, MGM also recorded an album of her *Transmutation* (1949) and *Two Chinese Songs* (1952), three albums of her four-piano arrangements, and two albums of piano pieces for children with Richter as pianist.[21] Through the recording process, Richter met a great number of artists interested in performing new music.

SONATA FOR PIANO (1954)

Richter's first large-scale concert work is her outstanding *Sonata for Piano*, composed in 1954. This difficult and sophisticated work is included in the widely used *Guide to the Pianist's Repertoire* by Maurice Hinson and described thusly: "A somber, often sinister mood permeates this work; and there is a sense of dark, forbidding power. [It uses] angular and dissonant harmonic language, compelling and demanding writing."[22]

At this time, in the early 1950s, although quite a few U.S. composers wrote piano sonatas (including Copland, Sessions, Carter, Ross Lee Finney, Kirchner, Krenek, Barber, David Diamond, Dello Joio, Persichetti, Ingolf Dahl, and George Walker), few U.S. women composed piano sonatas. Women composers of mid-century piano sonatas do include Louise Talma and Ruth Schonthal (U.S.), and Elisabeth Lutyens (English) and Grazyna Bacewicz (Polish). (As the 1960s approached, fewer piano sonatas were composed in general, as composers gravitated to more experimental music.)[23]

Richter's *Sonata for Piano* is highly chromatic, yet it elicits remnants of the formal structure of the classical form.[24] No key signatures are given for any of the movements, but through assertion and ostinatos, the three movements (fast-slow-fast) are tonally centered on E, C♯, and E, respectively. As in her *Sonata for Clarinet and Piano*, constant metric changes generate much energy. Richter writes idiomatically for the piano, always fitting the hand comfortably. She uses all three of the pedals sensitively, and expands the texture to four staves in some places. The piece is at times percussive, at times lyrical, and overall quite beautiful, within a highly chromatic language.

In the first movement, a modified sonata form, the slow mysterious introduction begins with unison notes derived from the octatonic scale: D, E, F, G, and G♯. The "ominous" exposition features rapid alternation between the hands as it gradually accelerates and crescendos. The climax of the movement, in the middle of the recapitulation, is a dramatic canon (on three staves). The second movement begins with a lyrical melody in the right hand accompanied by a left-hand arpeggio figure in minor ninths using the pitches C♯, D, D♯, and E. The melody is based on combinations of half and whole steps, with some minor ninths as well. Repeated notes, chords of fourths and sevenths, and tremolos in ninths successively accompany the melody. The movement eventually reaches a shattering climax and then subsides. The third movement is a fast virtuosic toccatalike movement marked "furioso." It is mostly in $\frac{5}{8}$ but has some changing meters. As in the opening movement, the piano is frequently used percussively and has much figuration that alternates rapidly between the hands.

In reviews of Menahem Pressler's 1956 MGM recording of the *Sonata*, much praise was given to Richter's sonata. Critic Elliot Zucherman commended the idiomatic writing for the instrument: "Marga Richter's Sonata is rich and powerful. Its large proportions and full use of every sort of piano technique place it, as she intended, in the tradition of the big sonatas of the nineteenth century."[25] Alfred Frankenstein admired its formal structure: "The sonata is a huge, formidable, complex and highly dramatic work, but one in which every usage is logically accounted for, and the whole adds up to an extremely vital and rewarding musical communication."[26] Composer Hall Overton extolled its distinctive personality in his *Metronome* review: "The Richter sonata is a big work, written in full bravura

7. Marga Richter, pianist Menahem Pressler, and Edward Cole, ca. 1955.

style for a pianist who is clearly a master of his instrument. Although it is frankly tonal at times, it resists such easy categorization through a free and individual use of dissonance."[27] John Rosenfield referred to it as "a bothersome [sonata]... [that] strikes us as all thorns."[28]

Much later, in 1978, when pianist Peter Basquin recorded the *Sonata* for Grenadilla Records, Richter's sonata again generated excitement by the reviewers. E. S. V. Leigh wrote: "It is a stark, lean, graceful work, absolutely bare of gimmicks or attractive contrivances, linear but yet savagely imaginative in pure, vibrant colors and dramatic, often angry, rhythms. Not only is there musical insight here, but poetic insight as well. This work is brilliantly descriptive of its time... Peter Basquin's performance is exceptional. Richter's Sonata was praised when first released in 1956, and has been recently rediscovered. This is the only modern recording of this work to date, one which I can recommend without qualification."[29] Composer and conductor Arthur Cohn wrote: "The playing of Peter Basquin is ideal for this work. He can sting a phrase and he does in the principal precipitancy of Marga Richter's music. Prissy pianism doesn't fit much music, least of all the rash adventure of this sonata."[30]

The work has continually garnered attention. Lenore Engdahl performed it on April 17, 1964, at an all-Richter concert at the Unitarian Universalist Fellowship of Huntington and again on October 13, 1984, in Carnegie Recital Hall. In November 1976 it was performed by Blanche Abram on a concert in Carnegie Recital Hall (along with works by other members of the Long Island Composers Alliance), and Peter G. Davis referred to it as a "rather ferociously gnarled, Lisztian" sonata in his review in the *New York Times*.[31] Vivian Taylor performed the sonata for the Museum of Modern Art's Summergarden series on July 16 and 17, 1976, and on a faculty lecture-recital on American women composers at Tufts University on April 3, 1977; she also played it at the Longy School of Music, Cambridge, Massachusetts (1979), Wigmore Hall, London (1981), Carnegie Recital Hall (1984), and again at Tufts University (1984). After the performance in Wigmore Hall (in the Purcell Room), a reviewer for the *London Daily Telegraph* wrote, "Pride of place had to go to Marga Richter's magnificent Sonata."[32] Other performers include Donald Kidd, Michael Skelly, Avraham Sternklar, and You Ju Lee.

In 2011 the sonata's third recording was released by Albany Records with Richard Zimdars as pianist. The recording also includes Richter's *Eight Pieces for Piano* and *Remembrances*, along with works by Vincent Persichetti and Jacob Druckman. In a review of this recording, critic Radu A. Lelutiu wrote:

> While they may not receive top billing, Marga Richter's works are in my view the real sleepers on this recording. In particular, the Sonata . . . reveals the mind of a fully realized master

composer. It is a whale of a piece—25 minutes in length—that makes enormous demands on the performer and the listener. Although the last movement bears a striking resemblance to Bartók, for the most part, Richter seems to have already found her voice. . . . I have no doubt that Richter's *Sonata* is one of the most important works written for the piano after 1950. To my ears, the meditative, neo-romantic *Remembrances* and the aphoristic Eight Pieces for Piano are not as impressive as the Sonata, but they add to the listener's understanding of Richter's musical interests and range.[33]

Music critic Michael Redmond has remarked specifically about the piano sonata:

> It's an uncompromising "Roger Sessions" kind of piece, but Marga Richter entirely. It's one of the most important piano sonatas from the 1950s, never mind that she's a woman—for me it's the music first. It has as much expression as a Liszt piece. I'm astounded that it's not better known. It's a big work, an important work.[34]

Clearly this sonata full of thorns makes an impression.

CONCERTO FOR PIANO AND VIOLAS, CELLOS AND BASSES (1955)

The success at large-scale composition that Richter experienced with her piano sonata continued with her first piano concerto, *Concerto for Piano and Violas, Cellos and Basses* (also called *Piano Concerto No. 1*) (1955). It was recorded in late 1956 for MGM by pianist William Masselos with Carlos Surinach conducting. Lawrence Sterne reviewed this recording saying:

> Miss Richter's choice of all the lower strings here results in tone colors of rather somber hues, yet she provides enough contrast to prevent saturation. Such a satisfying solution of a difficult scoring problem is only one of the signs of Miss Richter's mastery—and this concerto is full of them.[35]

The work was then premiered by pianist William Masselos with Gregory Millar conducting the San Francisco Little Symphony in 1957. Critic Alfred Frankenstein rhapsodized about the premiere:

> I do not recall hearing a new piano concerto with such keen interest since the second concerto of Ravel was unveiled. The strong tawny color of the piece is one of its special virtues; others are its wealth of modal-sounding melody, its crackling energy, and its shrewdly placed contrasts whereby a work of small proportions takes on large importance. Above everything, the concerto communicates a sense of adventure. It goes places. And so does the colossal virtuosity of Masselos.[36]

Critic Oliver Daniel wrote about the work:

> Wisconsin-born Marga Richter is obviously a fine and sensitive pianist, as previous record-

> ings indicate. Here she establishes herself as a composer and one of no mean gift. She has written a solid work and draws a big sound from her limited orchestra. She is able to be crashing without being a bore. But like many a lady composer she attacks the problem of music (at times) in an almost masculine way. The finest moments, and there are some truly beautiful ones, are those of a more gentle nature.
>
> Marga Richter is one of the young composers who bear watching.[37]

This comment on the work being "almost masculine" was echoed by other critics, one of whom described the concerto as "pungent and virile."[38] Another wrote: "Women composers are rare birds, to be sure, but one with as dissonant and biting a style as Marga Richter's is decidedly a shock. No Chaminade she, believe me; her masculine severity brings Honegger to mind."[39] At the time, she was flattered by such reviews, pleased to think "I'm as good as a guy."[40]

The concerto is in five movements (Moderato, Allegretto, Andante, Andante, and Allegro) without key signatures. The shorter movements two and four serve as transitions between the longer movements, one, three, and five. The piano part emphasizes melodic beauty somewhat more than in the piano sonata. Omitting the violins, Richter refreshingly explores the lower ranges and timbres of the string instruments. This sets off the piano part even more. Richter used the opening melody from the Kyrie of Bach's B Minor Mass to generate the main theme of the concerto's first movement.

Years later, in January 1976, conductor Ainslee Cox (1936–1988) and the Oklahoma Symphony Orchestra programmed this piano concerto with Richter as soloist.[41] Critic Nancy Gilson described the performance:

> Richter offered precision and grace to the unique and related movements of this intellectual yet mystery-filled piece. At the precise moment the Concerto appears to be a cool and almost technical work, the mood abruptly alters to intense drama and measured emotion.[42]

The work was also performed in February of 1976 by pianist Joel Salsman and the Northwest Chamber Orchestra in Seattle conducted by Louis Richmond, in 1979 by Richter's son Michael (see chapter 4). The work was premiered in England on November 8, 1988, with conductor Ruth Gipps.[43]

LAMENT FOR STRING ORCHESTRA (1956)

In November 1955 Richter learned from her father that her mother had been ill with cancer for some time. Being a Christian Scientist, her mother relied on her faith and her practitioner, and did not speak about it at all. In January of the next year, Richter went with five-month old Michael to Minneapolis to visit her (and to hear Lenore Engdahl play a piano concerto with the Minneapolis Symphony).

She and her mother did not acknowledge the certainty that this would be the last time they would see each other, and neither mentioned the illness. When Richter returned home she poured her unspoken feelings of the impending loss into composing her *Lament* for string orchestra. The very day she finished copying the last notes of the score, she received a phone call from her father that her mother had just died.

Shortly thereafter, the MGM orchestra recorded the work with Izler Solomon conducting. Critic Alfred Frankenstein described it as "a short piece of great eloquence, expressiveness, and harmonic subtlety."[44] In another review of the recording, critic Hall Overton wrote:

> The *Lament* shows a strong development toward simplicity and intensification which loses none of the dramatic power shown in the sonata but, in fact, increases it. The work is built in a pyramid design, rising steadily to a moving climax and gradually subsiding to the opening "dirge" music with a richly somber final cadence on E minor.[45]

Lament received its first public performance on November 14, 1971, on the University Museum Concert Series in Philadelphia. The Museum String Orchestra was conducted by William Smith, assistant conductor of the Philadelphia Orchestra. In an interview with Frances Harmeyer for Yale's Oral History of American Music (OHAM) project, Richter recalled:

> I finally got a performance in Philadelphia with William Smith, but only with a chamber group. It wasn't even part of the Philadelphia Orchestra. Once again, I came so close [to a performance by a world-class orchestra]. I thought: "Well, maybe he'll love it so much, he'll tell Ormandy about it"—because it would be tremendous for a person like Ormandy or Stokowski. I mean, I want to hear this piece with the massed strings of the ten greatest orchestras in the world out in Madison Square Garden. That's what this piece should be. Everybody in there should just have a catharsis. But what do *I* hear? I hear it with thirteen strings. It's all right, but it doesn't have any power. The MGM recording is all right, because you can beef it up a bit . . .
>
> I was sitting [in Philadelphia], listening in the audience, just weeping away. . . . The whole family came. Not only that, but two sets of our best friends happened to live there. . . . They all came. . . . Well, when it was finished none of them had a dry eye.[46]

The work was published by Broude Brothers (Rongwen Music) in 1958 as part of their Contemporary Composers study score series. (The same series included works by Ernst Krenek, Carlos Surinach, Alan Hovhaness, and Harold Farberman.)

On October 21, 1976, coincidentally Richter's fiftieth birthday, *Lament* did receive a performance by a large orchestra, the Minnesota Orchestra, conducted by Stanislaw Skrowaczewski.[47] Richter recalls that the occasion was extra special, as Irene Hellner was in the audience with Richter, who was carrying the hand-crocheted evening bag Hellner had made and given to Richter's mother.[48] Immediately after the performance, Skrowaczewski asked the orchestra manager to commission her. Although there was much communication between conductor and composer regarding a new work after this, Skrowaczewski left his post before this project came to fruition. They have kept in touch through the years, and in 2007 he wrote a letter of recommendation for her for a Guggenheim Fellowship.

Lament has also been performed by the National Gallery Orchestra conducted by Richard Bales in Washington, D.C. (1977), for the 34th American Music Festival, the Maracaibo Symphony in Venezuela, and the Eastern Music Festival Philharmonic conducted by Sheldon Morgenstern in Greensboro, North Carolina (July 23, 1977).

In a performance of *Lament* by the Garden State Chamber Orchestra on June 18, 1981, the conductor Frederick Storfer said to the audience, after having Richter take a bow, "I'm so moved by this piece I can hardly talk."[49]

In 1987, the Leonarda recording company produced a CD of orchestral works by U.S. women played by the Bournemouth Sinfonietta and the Arioso Chamber Orchestra, conducted by Carolann Martin. The CD includes Richter's *Lament*. Richter wrote for the liner notes:

8. Conductor Stanislaw Skrowaczewski with Marga Richter after performance of Lament, *1976.*

> [*Lament*] is built on a single quasi-modal theme, surrounded by sometimes dissonant counterpoint and ostinati. Growing slowly through a multiplicity of almost obsessive repetitions (which one conductor [William Smith] characterized as "mono-maniacal"), it reaches an intense climax, then subsides to a quiet ending.[50]

In a review of this CD Kenneth LaFave wrote:

> that Richter's consummate essay for string orchestra is back in the recorded repertoire is reason alone to cheer this CD. The main function of this recording should be to remind someone out there that this is a major work looking for its rightful place in the repertoire.[51]

Lament is a work of quiet grief, in a slow "Largo" $\frac{3}{4}$ meter, about eleven minutes long. It is without a key signature and is loosely based on E Dorian, with a G Phrygian section in the middle. Less dissonant than her other works from this time, *Lament* often has perfect fifths for harmony. It ends on an E minor triad.

ARIA AND TOCCATA FOR VIOLA AND STRING ORCHESTRA (1957)

In 1957 at the request of MGM records, Richter composed her *Aria and Toccata* for a recording by violist Walter Trampler with Carlos Surinach conducting the MGM String Orchestra. On March 8, 1957, Walter Trampler and Brooks Smith premiered a viola and piano version of *Aria and Toccata* in recital at the Coolidge Auditorium at the Library of Congress, and Trampler continued to play it in subsequent concerts. Other violists who have performed the work include Jacob Glick and Mimi Dye (with pianists Russell Miller and Camille Budarz). Reviewer Lawrence Sterne wrote "the solo instrument is set off against the string orchestra in ways that produce magical sound effects."[52] Edward Cole noted Richter's trademarks: "long-lined melody, an extraordinary sense of developmental architectonics, complexly dissonant harmony, [and] austere yet somehow super-charged emotionality."[53] Richter later used *Aria and Toccata* as the basis for her ballet, *Abyss* (see chapter 3).

TWO CHINESE SONGS (1952)

In 1952, Richter's continuing interest in Chinese poetry had resulted in her *Two Chinese Songs*: "The Hermit" and "Fishing Picture" to texts by Chinese poets (Li Hai-Ku and Ta-Chung-Kunkuang, translated by Amy Lowell and Florence Ayscough). The two songs have a simple, atmospheric beauty. "The Hermit" has a gentle and somewhat static two-part contrapuntal accompaniment emphasizing ninths and sevenths under a vocal line with a narrow range. "The Fishing Picture," in a lilting $\frac{6}{8}$ meter, uses some triads under a chromatically-inflected vocal line and ends on an open fifth.

These songs and her earlier *Transmutation* cycle (see chapter 1) were recorded by soprano Dorothy Renzi and pianist Maro Ajemian on an MGM album along with Pulitzer Prize winner Ernst Toch's *The Chinese Flute* (1923).

FOUR-PIANO ARRANGEMENTS

Richter was also engaged for hire by MGM to make four-piano arrangements of orchestral classics for three albums recorded by the Manhattan Piano Quartet, consisting of Lawrence Kruegar (aka Menahem Pressler), William Blankfort (aka William Masselos), Alexander Dickstein, and Marga Richter. The first album was *Tchaikovsky Waltzes*, seven in all, drawn from *Eugene Onegin*, *The Nutcracker*, *Serenade for Strings*, *Sleeping Beauty*, and *Swan Lake*. The second one was *Concert Favorites*, eight pieces including Khatchaturian's "Sabre Dance," Rimsky-Korsakov's "Flight of the Bumblebee," Wagner's *Ride of the Valkyries*, Mussorgsky's *Night on Bald Mountain* and *The Great Gate at Kiev*, Tchaikovsky's "Pas de Deux" and "Winter Scene" from *The Nutcracker*, and Humperdinck's "Dream Pantomime" from *Hansel and Gretel*. The third one, *Dances*, included dance pieces by Arthur Benjamin, Copland, Faure, Fernandez, Hovhaness, Jacoby, Kabalevsky, Lecuona, Mussorgsky, Offenbach, Shostakovich, and Weill. (On this album Elizabeth Olsen replaced the deceased Alexander Dickstein.)

Richter's arrangements of the Tchaikovsky waltzes drew special praise:

> Miss Richter's arrangements are clever and sometimes even ingenious in suggesting the original orchestrations, and her ideas are nimbly negotiated by the eight hands.[54]

> Their arrangements call for special mention. We have had piano quartets that sounded like two lead pianos, with two others filling in with non-essential frills. The Manhattan group sounds like a full orchestra with each piano of equal importance—a new and improved sound in piano quartets.[55]

PIECES FOR CHILDREN

In addition to these recordings, MGM produced two albums of Richter playing her own and other composers' children's piano pieces: *Piano Music for Children by Modern American Composers* and *Piano Music for Children by Modern Composers*.

On the first of these, Richter recorded her *Two Short Suites for Young Pianists* (1949, 1954), each suite containing three movements: *Angry*, *Melancholy*, and *Joyful* in Suite 1; and *Raindrops*, *Lullaby*, and *Hiccups* in Suite 2. All the movements in both suites are in five-finger positions except *Hiccups*. Much like Bartók's teaching pieces, these short works are richly constructed and introduce students to staccato and legato, voice exchanges, contrary motion, intervallic diminution, bitonality, ostinatos, irregular and mixed meters, and pentatonic and modal scales. (Richter did not return to writing teaching pieces until 1970.) Other composers on the album include Copland, Cowell, Diamond, Persichetti, Harold Lawrence, Alan Skelly, Stanley Wolfe, and Virgil Thompson. On the *Modern Composers* album were Hindemith, Hovhaness, Satie, Surinach, and Toch.

Not only were Richter's suites admired, but her playing on both albums received high praise as well. From a review of the *Modern American Composers* album: "Everything on the record is performed with infinite care and seriousness of purpose by a pianist of artistic stature."[56] From two reviews of the *Modern Composers* album: "Miss Richter plays all with a deep sense of purpose, technical skill and an infectious abandon."[57] And "It is played here by Marga Richter, who, needless to say, is no student but a top virtuoso. She makes it into a captivating listening experience while showing the novices how it can and should sound."[58]

The MGM series of recordings marked an exciting period of success in Richter's life. Numerous other works were composed during this time that, although not recorded, received performances.

Other Works from This Time

Also in the 1950s, Richter wrote a number of shorter compositions. *Nocturne for Sara Lee* (1953) was composed for one of her piano students. It is a gentle, short ABA work, using only *p* and *pp* for dynamics, mostly in Aeolian mode with some chromaticism. The middle section's melody places right-hand second inversion major and minor triads against an eighth-note arpeggiated left hand.[59]

In 1954 Richter composed *She, At His Funeral* for soprano and piano to a poem by the English novelist and poet Thomas Hardy (1840–1928). (Hardy's *Tess of the d'Urbervilles* would later inspire her *Spectral Chimes/Enshrouded Hills*, see chapter 5.) This was the last solo song she composed until the 1980s, although she did write choral music. Richter captures the dirge text with a simple melodic line accompanied by fifths, fourths, and continuous tolling on a repeated note throughout the piece. The piece is centered on A and starts with an inverted pedal tone on A. The climax comes with the line, "But they stand round with griefless eyes whilst my regret consumes like fire." The singer's line rises through a D harmonic minor scale against chromatic chords in the piano until C♯ on "fire," then dies away chromatically. A subdued piano postlude ends the song on an A–E♭ tritone.

Later, in 1976, Richter met soprano Jessye Norman at a Long Island Chamber Ensemble Concert in Hempstead, Long Island. Richter sent a copy of *She, At His Funeral* to Norman, who wrote back in a letter, "It is an exceptionally beautiful song. I would be honoured to perform it. May I let you know when I plan to do so? Thank you very much. Very best regards."[60] In a conversation Richter had with Jessye Norman after her Carnegie Hall performance in the fall of 1977, Norman told Richter she had performed her song, *She, At His Funeral*, in London in the spring. The concert was devoted to U.S. composers.

THREE SONGS OF MADNESS AND DEATH

Richter also contributed to the choral literature with her earliest work for chorus, *Three Songs of Madness and Death* (unaccompanied SATB chorus; 1954–55). The texts are from three novels by London playwright John Webster (ca. 1580–ca. 1638): "A Dirge" from *The White Devil*, "All the Flowers of Spring" from *The Devil's Law-Case*, and "Madman's Song" from *The Duchess of Malfi*. Webster was a late contemporary of Shakespeare and is known for his bleak, pessimistic writing.

Repetition of phrases and rhythmic ostinatos are the musical basis of the three short pieces. None of the three pieces has a key signature, and each is divided into sections with each section featuring a particular interval, often a fourth or fifth. These works are effective in performance and rather light in nature considering the subject matter. Their emphasis on chromatic lines, interval sets, and textural contrasts is characteristic of Richter's musical language.

Joseph Liebling conducted the New York Chamber Chorus of the Master Singers in the premiere of the work at the 92nd Street YM-YWHA on February 16, 1958, as part of the influential Max Pollikoff series "Music in Our Time: 1900–1958." Richter was the only female on the program that included works by Samuel Barber, William Bergsma, Robert Kurka, and Arnold Schoenberg.

MELODRAMA (1956–58)

A fun work by Richter (most of her works are quite serious in mood) is her 1956 *Melodrama* for two pianos. To create *Melodrama* she removed the percussion part from her 1953 comic ballet score, *The Vagabonds*, and greatly expanded the variations movement. The six movements are: Prologue, The Chase, Boy—Girl Dance, Inching-Out Dance (a Sarabande theme with 9 variations), Work Dance, and Finale—The Escape.

Richter describes the plot that inspired both the original ballet and this derivative work:

> The story begins with a band of carefree vagabonds being roused from their morning slumbers by the proverbial "villain" who chases them off his land. A boy from outside the group meets one of the girls and they fall in love. The boy is drawn into, then eased out of, the

> group during a stately Sarabande and variations. Later he rejoins them to help build a rocket-ship in which they make their final escape from the villain, just in the nick of time.[61]

She continues, "In keeping with the light-hearted naiveté of the plot, the music is simple, direct and accessible melodically and harmonically."[62]

Though they did not perform it, the work was dedicated to a famous duo piano team at the time, Ethel Bartlett and Rae Robertson. The work was, however, premiered eight years later on April 17, 1964, at the Unitarian Fellowship Hall in Huntington, New York, by pianists Jean Vandersall and Barbara Kupferberg (see chapter 3). Both Vandersall and Kupferberg were part of a piano group that Richter had formed on Long Island. (Richter had also formed a group like this when she was at Juilliard.) The Long Island piano group met monthly, except in summers, for about thirty years and played pieces for each other. Richter usually played her own compositions.

Other piano duos that have performed *Melodrama* are Marga Richter and Avraham Sternklar (Huntington, Roslyn, and Plainview, N.Y.); Lydia Hailparn and Avraham Sternklar (Madison, N.J., and Lewisburg, Pa.); Shirley Moore and Betty Nolling (Atlanta); Vivian Taylor and John McDonald (Medford, Mass.); and Marilyn Lehman Sherman and Adrienne Borbely (Garden City, N.Y.).

Richter has also performed *Melodrama* with her son Michael Skelly on several occasions, including performances at Tufts and Drew Universities. Skelly remarks:

> Anyone who comes to her music through that piece is going to find that there aren't a whole lot of other pieces by her that are very much like that. It's almost completely tonal at almost every moment, among other things. I think that piece is great fun. We had a lot of fun doing that. There are sections that are a little harder than I would have liked, but that's okay.[63]

STRING QUARTET NO. 2 (1958)

Another work that borrows from an earlier dance score, *The Wanderers*, is Richter's *String Quartet No. 2* (1958). About fifteen minutes long and comprised of two movements, a prelude "Largo" and a triple fugue "Andante Sostenuto-Allegro-Presto-Allegro," it utilizes all of the viable music from that score as thematic material in the fugue.[64]

The Max Pollicoff Quartet premiered Richter's *String Quartet No. 2* (1958) at the Bennington Composer Conference in Vermont in 1960 (see chapter 3). The work has received numerous performances over the years. Critic Mark Acheson wrote about one performance:

> It is a work of stature and technical ability free of academic restraint. It would be a pleasure to hear it again and again, for I am sure there is much to discover in its rich soil.[65]

A 1973 review of a Buffalo, New York, performance of the *String Quartet No. 2* compared the work to Messiaen and Ives.[66]

In 2000 the Meridian String Quartet, the quartet-in-residence at Queens College (New York), recorded the work for a CD of U.S. quartets composed between 1958 and 1999. According to Richter's liner notes for this CD,

> The prelude is very slow and has two contrasting elements: a continuous winding and highly chromatic melody in the first violin and a 4-note diatonic motif which appears in every bar in one or more voices and functions as a movable ostinato. The movement ends on a pianissimo implied a-minor ninth chord. The opening bars of the fugue provide the resolution, both by beginning in d-minor and by using the first three notes of the prelude's "ostinato" as the head of its first subject. The rest of the 8-bar theme features wide chromatic leaps while retaining its modal character. The second subject appears about half-way through the fugue. It is faster and livelier than the first and features repeated staccato notes (used to prefigure the actual first entrance) which easily cut through the often dense counterpoint. The third subject uses all of the notes of the first subject but in equal time-values (triplet eighths). This subject comes in about two-thirds of the way through the movement and from there to the end all three subjects and the ostinato material vie for attention in a virtual free-for-all.[67]

RICERCARE, FOR STRING QUARTET (1958)

In 1958 Richter was commissioned by Carl Fischer to write a piece for string quartet using only first position, for use in public schools. For this she composed her *Ricercare*, for string quartet. She composed the nine-measure theme while holding and nursing baby Maureen.

A very practical piece for students, it clearly opens and closes in C minor, without a key signature. In ricercare style, the subject enters in the first violin part, is answered at the fifth in the cello, followed by an entry on D in the viola, and on A in the second violin. The work demonstrates Richter's skill at writing high-quality music for student musicians.

She then arranged *Ricercare* for brass quartet (two trumpets, French horn and trombone or tuba), for The Long Island Brass Ensemble which premiered it at the Hicksville Public Library on Long Island on December 20, 1959. William Kupferberg, trombonist of the ensemble, then asked her to arrange it for the Westbury (L.I.) High School Band, of which he was the conductor. It was premiered there on May 26, 1960.

VARIATIONS ON A SARABANDE, FOR ORCHESTRA

In 1959 Richter orchestrated the fourth movement of her light-hearted *Melodrama*, entitling it *Variations on a Sarabande*. The work was premiered on November 2, 1961, by conductor Thomas Nee and the Civic Orchestra of Minneapolis, and received later performances by the Vermont Philharmonic with Brian Webb, conductor; the Haddonfield Symphony with Arthur Cohn; the Fox Valley Symphony (Appleton, Wisc.) with Kate Tamarkin; and a number of community and high school orchestras, including the Huntington High School Orchestra conducted by Thomas Karolyi. Richter's two children were members of the orchestra at the time, Michael on bassoon and Maureen on cello. Richter recalls with good humor that, because some of the orchestra members were less than enthusiastic about the music and made derogatory remarks, Maureen and Michael Skelly did not acknowledge their relationship to Marga Richter.[68]

Richter's program note details the intricate contrapuntal structure of the variations:

> The piece is a set of nine variations on an original theme in the Dorian mode, which is stated at the outset by a brass quintet. Most of the variations follow the basic harmonic structure which accompanies the theme, and the contours of the original melody remain for the most part readily apparent. Variation II, however, presents the theme in an exact inversion against a chromatically descending figure in the strings; Variation V is built on both the original and inverted forms played simultaneously; and Variation VIII introduces entirely new, sharply rhythmic figures against a very strong brass statement of a slightly simplified version of the theme.[69]

In a review of the Minneapolis performance, critic John Sherman wrote, "Mastery of orchestral color and thematic manipulation were major attributes here, and the orchestra gave them full value."[70]

The 1950s were exciting years for Richter. Initially she lived a somewhat uninhibited lifestyle in the chicken house (New Paltz) and in Greenwich Village, enjoying the company of fellow artists and achieving significant success with her modern dance scores and MGM recordings. She did follow some of the conventions of the day with marriage and raising children at home but steadfastly continued to pursue her career.

3 Fragments
1960s

> *Lament* might be my favorite. I absolutely love that work. I think I love all of her music. She's always made the point that music is an emotional and spiritual thing. During that whole twelve-tone scene, she always said music is emotionally driven. It has to say something to you. It can't just be an intellectual exercise. I think that's why her music speaks to people. Because it comes out of a place of inspiration. I think first she always gets the inspiration and then she writes the piece.
>
> Maureen Skelly Raj, interview by Sharon Mirchandani, 2008

U.S. COMPOSERS IN THE 1960s (e.g., Carter, Varèse, Babbitt, and Cage) gravitated toward total serialism, electronic music, or chance music. Richter never found these styles appealing and did not adopt them. She did reluctantly respond to the trend of composing sparse, economical, and atonal works. She began to compose shorter, more fragmented works that had little or no development and were not as expansive as her earlier (and later) works.

The added responsibilities of motherhood may have also encouraged shorter works, although Richter said she did not consider this a factor in her compositional decisions and never viewed motherhood as an impediment to her creative work. She hired sitters for several hours each day when the children were very young in order to work without interruption. She brought work with her on vacation at a time when most women did not. Quite helpful was the support she received from her husband and children.

In 1960 Richter's *String Quartet No. 2* (1958, see chapter 2) was premiered by the Max Pollicoff Quartet at the Bennington Composers Conference in Vermont.[1] Richter's remarks reveal her ambivalence about her experiences at Bennington:

> It was a summer thing and composers would go. You had to be accepted, and you had to pay something, and you'd go and you'd get a work rehearsed and recorded. A friend of

9. Marga Richter with daughter Maureen and son Michael, 1968.

> mine said, "you should really go there," and I thought I've never applied to MacDowell, or Yaddo or any of these places, because I don't need another place to work, although it'd be good because you meet other people, but I just never did it. I could still do it now and meet some people, I suppose, but I have places to work, and I'm happy the way I am, so . . . I probably missed out on that. But you'd only do what you [already] do, right? . . . I brought my *Second String Quartet*, and they actually played that. They also played the beginning of what I was going to call a symphony, but it was like two-part counterpoint *[laughs]* . . . it was so simple, there wasn't any point in having them play it [but] they did.[2]

Richter generally preferred her independence and isolation to a large extent, not feeling a strong need to network with other composers.

However, one encounter at the Bennington Composers Conference, with composer William Sydeman (b. 1928), was influential in steering her toward the prevailing attitudes of the day. Richter describes this:

> Up there I met this composer named William Sydeman. And I remember bringing a recording of my first piano concerto and playing it for him, thinking he would be really knocked out. But, he didn't like it, because it was too . . . I won't use the word 'ordinary,' but it didn't do anything

> spectacularly different in form or anything like that, it was just a nice emotional piece. He was nice about it, but I could see that he thought it was boring. [He said] 'You should really think in terms of conciseness. Don't develop it so much, don't be so obvious . . . '—that kind of thing. He didn't use those terms, but I think he probably knew I knew what he thought. This piece was too mainstream. Since I liked him a lot, I thought maybe I should try that. I was influenced by him for about five years. I wrote pieces like *Fragments*, *Eight Pieces for Orchestra* and the piano version, *Soundings*, and my *Suite for Violin and Piano*. Plus a chamber piece which was premiered at Yale but which is really terrible and has been withdrawn from my catalog. So I went off on that kick for awhile. And then I got sick of it, because it just wasn't me. I mean, those pieces are still me, but they're not really representative.[3]

Richter's remarks here suggest that her discomfort in trying to write more concise pieces may have inhibited her production more than did motherhood.

Miniatures

The most important of these short solo and chamber works from the 1960s are *Eight Pieces for Piano* (1960), *Eight Pieces for Orchestra* (1961–62), *Darkening of the Light* for solo viola (1962, cello 1976), *Fragments* for piano (1963, orch. 1978), *Suite for Violin and Piano* (1963), and *Soundings* for harpsichord (1965). Minor works composed during this time are *Chamber Piece* (for flute, oboe, clarinet, bassoon, viola, cello, bass) (1961), *Three Pieces* for violin and piano (1961) composed for Stephen Salinger, *A Farewell* for piano (1961), and *The Lost People* and *The Dancers* for piano (1968) composed for her daughter Maureen.

EIGHT PIECES FOR PIANO (1960)

Maurice Hinson describes *Eight Pieces* in *Guide to the Pianist's Repertoire* as "short, [using] contemporary techniques, expressionistic."[4] Richter premiered the work in New York City on February 28, 1975.

Richter's description of their genesis provides insight into the compositional world at that time. As she describes it, she was trying to avoid being "obvious" partly in response to the Sydeman suggestion and partly because it seemed an interesting approach to experiment with. The pieces are very short, only about a minute long, and have little or no development. Richter continued, "So, I thought I'd try something different. That's why I wrote those *Eight Pieces*. I just sat down, and wrote whatever came to my head. As soon as it wasn't in my head anymore, or my fingers, I quit. . . . I thought: 'Well, that's fun. That's really fun. You know, you can really say a lot.'"[5]

A recurring three-note motive in several of the pieces, consisting of an ascending minor third followed by either an ascending or descending minor second (or with slight variations) is used to haunting effect and unifies the set. The pieces are dissonant and pointillistic in style.

EIGHT PIECES FOR ORCHESTRA (1961–62)

Richter studied orchestration with Sydeman for a few months at Mannes College and this prompted her to arrange the *Eight Pieces* for piano for large orchestra in 1961–62. In addition to pairs of flutes, oboes, clarinets, bassoons, and five-part strings, she used piccolo, English Horn, bass clarinet, contra bassoon, four horns, three trumpets, three trombones, tuba, four timpani, bass drum, harp, celesta, and piano. She described feeling as though she were going from watercolor to oil.

The orchestral version of *Eight Pieces* was performed on Long Island in 1969 by the Huntington Symphony conducted by Seymour Lipkin. The performance received an excellent review by Dr. Russell Bliss, assistant professor of music at Nassau Community College. (Richter would later teach for a short while at Nassau Community College.) Bliss wrote:

> That a composer of Marga Richter's stature lives in Huntington is cause for rejoicing; that she is little known nationally is cause for wonder; that the orchestra brilliantly performed her *Eight Pieces* should make us all proud. Her music is craggy, uncompromising and profound; it is fresh and fascinating; it is beautiful. Its sound is dissonant but not atonal, its style is laconic-nearly pointillist, but not serial. She handles a large and complex orchestra with utmost assurance—always achieving a sought-after effect with precision.
>
> Especially effective was the use of harp and celesta in the fifth piece and the cello melody in Number 7 against which a clarinet and a piccolo—not a flute, mind you—made brief commentary. The playing time for the eight pieces was slightly under five minutes—like Japanese Haiku poetry they are brief but pungent—so Mr. Lipkin wisely and generously repeated them on the spot. The orchestra was at its best in this performance, the music was projected with vivid power and understanding and make no mistake, these pieces are fiendishly difficult to make sound.[6]

Though not serial, these brief works really show the Webern-inspired pointillistic style that was so widespread during the 1960s in the United States. They focus on a sparse texture and color above all else.

DARKENING OF THE LIGHT FOR SOLO VIOLA (1962)

Originally titled "Suite for Solo Viola," *Darkening of the Light* consists of nine short interrelated movements building, archlike, from a quiet, melancholy opening to a free rhapsodic outburst, and then ending quietly. Richter changed the title when it was published by Carl Fischer in a facsimile edition (FE134), based on lines from the *I Ching: Hexagram No. 36*, which her husband Alan brought to her attention:

> The light has sunk into the earth:
> The image of Darkening of the Light.
> Wounding of the Bright.
> The light is veiled, yet still shines.[7]

The short acerbic movements of the piece seem well-characterized by these lines. The work was premiered on January 11, 1967, by Jacob Glick at the Library and Museum of the Performing Arts, Lincoln Center, and has received numerous later performances including those by Glick, Karen Phillips, Patricia McCarty, Ken Edwards, Christine Ims, Ruth Siegler, Suzanne Valerio, and Jonathan Weber. In 1976 Richter transcribed the piece for cello.

FRAGMENTS FOR PIANO (1963)

Richter continued to use combinations of ascending and descending thirds and seconds as in the *Eight Pieces* in her five-movement *Fragments*. The pieces in this set are even briefer than those in *Eight Pieces*. They are also less jagged and more lyrical. Richter premiered her five-movement *Fragments* in Huntington, New York, on April 17, 1964.

In 1978 Richter arranged *Fragments* for a standard orchestra, using pairs of flutes, oboes, clarinets, bassoons, and horns, as well as piccolo, bass clarinet, trumpet, trombone, tuba, timpani, tenor drum, bass drum, suspended cymbal, and five-part strings. She also included harp and celesta. This work was premiered on April 30, 1986, by Paul Phillips and the Greensboro Youth Symphony.

SUITE FOR VIOLIN AND PIANO (1963)

Richter's *Suite for Violin and Piano* consists of five brief and highly dissonant movements. The first is for muted violin alone and leads directly into the second movement in which the piano enters with damper and una corda pedals held down throughout. The third movement is a march, the fourth is a lament, and the final movement is a more complex extended marchlike risoluto movement with complex rhythms such as sextuplets against sixteenths. The work was premiered by Jo Margaret Farris, violin, and Richter in Huntington on April 17, 1964.

SOUNDINGS FOR HARPSICHORD (1965)

Soundings, a delicate and intricate work in five short movements, was commissioned by and composed for harpsichordist Ilse Foerstel Bliss, who premiered it in

February 1967 at the Unitarian Fellowship Hall in Huntington. Richter describes it in her amusing program note:

> This short piece demands not only a virtuoso performer, but a virtuoso harpsichord. There are a number of split-second registration changes which call for great skill from the artist and great cooperation from the instrument.[8]

In the 1970s harpsichordist Sonia Gezairlian Grib championed *Soundings*, including it frequently on her recitals. She performed it on the 1981 all-Richter concert in Merkin Hall, New York City, at which time Richter provided the following program note:

> It is in five short inter-related movements: Slow-Fast-Slow-Fast-Slow. The opening movement combines austere, essentially melodic material with sudden outbursts of sound. It is a capsulized preview of the entire work, its apparently unrelated fragments developed separately in the later movements. The fourth and fifth movements also draw on an additional source of material, the last movement of Beethoven's Sonata in E Major, Opus 109. It is first hinted at in the fourth movement in the form of brief tremolos in thirds and slow chromatic turns. The fifth movement contains recurrent suggestions of the opening bars of the Beethoven which escalate in intensity. The culmination of the piece is a literal but skeletal utterance of the first two bars of the Beethoven theme, closing on the dominant chord of B Major whose bass gives way to a low A and thereby, in effect, suspends the musical structure indefinitely.[9]

The concert was reviewed by Theodore Libbey Jr. for the *New York Times*: "The program opened with 'Soundings,' an attractive, lightly textured work for harpsichord, which does a particularly good job of exploring the instrument's touch and decay."[10] *Soundings* does exploit the nondampened ring of the harpsichord, and its texture is thin, always two-part or monophonic. It is a freely atonal work, without key signatures, and has the feeling of improvisation with a great deal of rhythmic fluctuation, at times using quintuplets, septuplets, nonets, and seven-against-three patterns.

Variations on a Theme by Latimer for Piano Four-Hands (1964)

The roots of *Variations on a Theme by Latimer* go back to Richter's 1952 dance score *Johnny Got His Gun*. Richter's friend Phyllis Latimer was writing a symphony that Richter liked, and Richter used one of its themes for the theme-and-variations movement in the dance score. Latimer once observed that the diatonic half of the theme was hers, but the more interesting chromatic half of the theme was Richter's.[11]

In 1964 Richter arranged this movement for piano four-hands, adding additional material. The work consists of an eight-measure lyrical theme and eight variations of greatly varying lengths (from 16 to 73 measures) and intensity. Premiered by Richter and Barbara Kupferberg at the April 17, 1964, concert, it has also been performed by the sister duo Nanette Kaplan Solomon and Iris Kaplan; Lucille Felsenthal and Jean Vandersall; Richter and her son Michael Skelly; Iris Wenglin and composer Ruth Lomon; and Rebecca Jeffers and Angela Carlson, among others.

On April 17, 1964, an all-Richter concert was performed at the Unitarian Universalist Fellowship Hall in Huntington. In addition to her *Variations on a Theme by Latimer* (Richter/Kupferberg), other premieres on this concert (which also included Engdahl's performance of *Sonata for Piano*) were her 1956 *Melodrama* for two pianos (Vandersall/Kupferberg), *Fragments* (Richter), and *Suite for Violin and Piano* (Jo Margaret Farris/Richter). Robert Lee Tipps reviewed the concert for the *Long Islander*:

> Few contemporary composers seem as willing to commit their lives and talents to creating that which they feel they must say. Flowing through her works are two factors which place them in the immediate present, a sense of restlessness and an enormous amount of musical tension. She can, within the compass of a single form, create an icy atmosphere reminiscent of Sibelius, a nightlike eeriness found in Bartók, or a great burst of rage like that filling the more massive works of Beethoven.[12]

Eight-year-old Michael Skelly turned pages for *Variations on a Theme by Latimer*.

Three Choral Works

During the 1960s, Richter also began composing more choral works: *Psalm 91* for mixed chorus (1962), *Three Songs for Christmas* for children's chorus (1964), and *Seek Him* for mixed chorus (1965). These works are more modal and somewhat less dissonant than her instrumental compositions.

PSALM 91

Richter's 1962 setting, *Psalm 91* (unaccompanied SATB chorus), was commissioned and premiered by the First Presbyterian Church of Oyster Bay, New York (her first paid commission—$30!). It was later performed at the American Society of University Composers 1977 Region 2 conference at Cornell University by the Thomas Sokol Chorale, and by the Nassau Community College chorus, Richard Keggereis conducting. The setting uses verses 1–4 and 9–11 of the sixteen verses of the psalm. No meter (or key signature) is provided, rather the indication "slowly, in the manner of Gregorian Chant" is given and the measures vary from four to eight beats. Constantly shifting textures are used to create motion. The piece moves from a three-voice texture that suggests aeolian mode to four voices that are more chromatic, back to three again, and ends with just two voices (soprano and alto) on a sustained major second. The soprano is frequently in octaves with the tenor or bass. Nearly all of the motion is stepwise with the emphasis on the weaving lines. Imitation provides textural contrast and a feeling of strength in verse 9 with the words, "Because thou hast made the Lord, which is my refuge, even the Most High, thy habitation."

THREE SONGS FOR CHRISTMAS

In 1964 Richter wrote *Three Songs for Christmas* (SA, two flutes or piano) for the Huntington Children's Chorus. Whereas the pieces contain chromaticism, they do have key signatures and are modal. No. 1, "Christmas Song," poem by Eugene Field (1850–1895), has a lively ostinato in the choir, sometimes in imitation, that is supported by the flutes (or piano). A soprano soloist carries the main text, in sustained half notes above the ostinato. The piece is mostly in F-sharp minor; at the end it moves to A major and ends on the dominant chord. No. 2, "Cradle Hymn," poem by Isaac Watts (1674–1742), is in a lilting $\frac{6}{8}$ meter in E Dorian. No. 3, "Christmas Carol," to a poem by Phillips Brooks (1835–1893), in G mixolydian mode, is the most challenging of the three. It calls on the performers to sing in parallel perfect fourths, has frequent tempo changes, and sections in free imitation. The texts (especially attractive to children) address bells and singing, blessings and the manger, and the earth's "soul full of music."

SEEK HIM

Choral composition continued as an important part of Richter's oeuvre with *Seek Him* (SATB) (1965), a setting of Amos 5:8. One of her most frequently performed choral works, the piece is a strong, declamatory statement that pits stark open fifths and fourths against more sinewy chromatic melodic lines. Again, Richter uses textural and intervallic contrast to express each line of text. She has sections based on the major tetrachord, the octatonic scale, octaves, and minor sixths. Free imitation contrasts with paired voices in dialogue. The piece ends powerfully with chords in open fifths and fourths only. This was Richter's last choral work until 1980. The second half of the decade saw a return to writing dramatic large-scale works.

Works for the Harkness Ballet

An important acknowledgment of the power of Richter's craft came with the commissioning of her modern ballet score, *Abyss* (1964–65), by the Harkness Ballet.

In the fall of 1964, choreographer Stuart Hodes, a former principal dancer with the Martha Graham Dance Company (and later dean of students of the Martha Graham School of Contemporary Dance), phoned Richter, said he loved the recording of her *Aria and Toccata* and would like to choreograph a dance to it based on Leonid Andreyev's story *Abyss* for the Harkness Ballet, and asked if she would be interested in working with him. Richter responded with an emphatic "Yes!" Because Hodes needed an additional ten minutes between the aria and the toccata, he arranged for a commission from the Harkness Foundation.

Richter recalls:

> When I met with their representative to discuss the fee and was offered $1,000 ("We gave Samuel Barber $1,500 for 15 minutes, so . . .") my inner "little-girl-from-Robbinsdale" blushed and blurted out "What?!" For this section I worked closely with Stuart to compose music to match the narrative and movements. He then matched the choreography to the flow and shape of the music. We used the *Aria* as it was (solo viola and strings), and I transcribed the *Toccata* for full orchestra.[13]

The premiere took place in Cannes on February 27, 1965. In an April 2, 1965, article in *Time* magazine about the new Harkness Ballet's first season, the critics singled out *Abyss* (then called *The Abyss*) and two ballets by Alvin Ailey as the most successful offerings. The Harkness Ballet subsequently performed it in Paris, Hamburg, Lisbon, Monaco, and other cities in Europe, North Africa, and North and South America.

Richter recounts the circumstances of attending her first performance of the ballet:

> I had not seen the ballet yet, because they hadn't come to New York. It was being done in Washington, D.C. [in the fall of 1966], and I was having an orchestration lesson that day with Stanley Hollingsworth in New York [courtesy of Rebekah Harkness]. About two o'clock in the afternoon, Mrs. Harkness . . . I don't think she came herself to tell me, but she sent a message that I should go to Washington and see the ballet, and she would provide the airline ticket and everything. The first thought was, "I'm not dressed." The second thought . . . I had a run in my stockings. So I went out to Woolworth's and bought some stockings. I took the plane. I got myself to La Guardia . . . I got to the airport in Washington. I'm not good at any of that . . . (and I don't remember how I got myself home). . . . In those days I always wore cologne when I went "out." But I wasn't wearing any that day. So I went to the perfume counter at the airport where they sell the stuff. I wanted Arpège, it cost $6 . . . I did not want to spend $6 . . . I told the sales woman what was happening (seeing, hearing the ballet) and she said "lean over" and she sprayed me and off I went. I had to stand in the back [of the theater]—can you believe it? I did not have a seat to watch my ballet.

Richter attended the New York premiere in November 1967 at the Broadway Theatre. She also attended their second New York engagement at the Music Box Theatre in November 1969. The following anecdote shows her dogged determination to always try to make things better:

> A few years later they did do it in New York. By that time I had changed the ending a couple of times. They did it three nights in a row, and I went to the first performance and I didn't think it was good enough and I went home and thought "This is just not right." I changed a few horn notes and something with the rhythm and I went back to the orchestra pit and I went right down there and changed the notes for the players. It was a simple thing, but it was the rhythm. And I went backstage at intermission and I said to the conductor, "It's going to be like this," and he said, "I can't do that," and I said, "Yes, you can," and he did it. He just changed the whole thing right there on the spot [rechoreographing for the dancers]. It was pretty exciting.[14]

In 1966, reviewer Alexander Fried wrote of a Harkness performance in San Francisco at the Geary Theater: "Marga Richter's music totally sustained the mood of the story."[15] However, in several reviews of *Abyss* from this time, the *New York Times* dance critic Clive Barnes does not mention Richter. This annoyed the composer, who wrote him an amusing letter in February of 1967 gently complaining about the omission and requesting that he at least mention her name.

> Dear Mr. Barnes, I should like to bring to your attention what I hope is an unintentional oversight. In your Cannes, Paris, and now, Washington reviews of *Abyss*, you have consistently failed to mention my name as composer of the score. I am sure you can understand how such neglect can begin to bother a person, especially when all the other composers are listed.
>
> This week I suffered two such omissions, first by Mr. Terry [critic Walter Terry], and then by yourself. I can remain silent no longer, as my indifference to fame is not that great. If you have an aversion to my music, perhaps I benefit from *your* silence—but I am now willing to take that chance. Please, Mr. Barnes, next time, mention my name?
>
> A few weeks ago I was going to send you a fan letter (willing to blot the ignominious past from my consciousness) telling you how much I enjoy reading your column—read it regularly, not because I care that much about the dance-world, but because I find your ideas provocative and your style delicious and amusing.
>
> I have recently become a music critic for the local paper, and with you as a model have taken courage to write what I really think and feel about performances, about performing, about the Huntington Symphony (you have to be a little bit gentle with a semi-professional community orchestra) and even had the temerity to suggest a few judicious cuts in an overlong Schubert Symphony. Heresy. I also wrote a 750-word review in which I forgot to mention the conductor. So I know how it is.
>
> Being a composer, especially a woman-composer, is a slightly masochistic activity, but my case is not severe enough to cause my giving up the pleasure of reading your reviews. However, I may give up writing for the Dance. Sincerely, yours, Marga Richter[16]

Perhaps in response, Barnes wrote in his November 1967 review of a Harkness *Abyss* performance, "The choreography . . . is helped by the somber atmosphere of Marga Richter's music." However, in his 1971 review of *Abyss*, he cuttingly wrote, "The music by Marga Richter is blandly anonymous music that is quite extraordinarily forgettable" and again does not mention her in a 1974 review of a performance by the Joffrey Ballet.[17]

In 1976, Richter felt somewhat vindicated when *Abyss* was performed in a concert version with Roland Johnson conducting the Madison Symphony Orchestra in Wisconsin, and, in an extended review, David Wagner praised the music:

> There is no doubt about its success as a concert piece. Particularly striking and beautiful Saturday night was the first part, a lyrical viola solo performed over the muted accompaniment of all the other string players in the orchestra by principal violist Sheila Magnuson.
>
> It is rare enough for a viola to take such an extended solo, and Magnuson performed it with an equally rare sensitivity both in the higher reaches of the instrument and especially in the dark, resonant bottom tones, which anticipated with appropriate foreboding the fate of the lovers following the pas de deux which it describes.
>
> . . . After the viola solo much of the piece is devoted to the rhythmic requirements of the choreographer, but the Stravinskian touches with which those requirements are fulfilled are never crudely imitative. The entire work has an independent musical force, and clearly belongs in the standard orchestral repertoire.[18]

In addition to the Joffrey, other ballet companies that mounted *Abyss* included the Boston, Pennsylvania, and Connecticut companies. In a review of a Connecticut performance, Ernestine Stodelle wrote, "Even Marga Richter's music, which I found harshly dissonant at times, seems to belong dynamically to the dramatic action."[19]

BIRD OF YEARNING (1967)

The great success of *Abyss* prompted the Harkness Ballet to commission Hodes and Richter to create a second work. Originally titled *The Servant*, based on the Russian tale by S. T. Semyonov, it was premiered in Cologne in 1969 as *Der Turm* (The tower); subsequently the title was changed again, this time to *Bird of Yearning*. Richter used some of her piece *Fragments* in it, but she does not view this ballet music as "viable."

Vermont—A Compositional Retreat

In 1964, Richter and her husband purchased an eighty-acre property in Shrewsbury, Vermont, and spent summers there, camping, until they could have their prefabricated vacation house constructed in 1969. Once the house was erected, they spent about two years finishing the interior themselves. They had the essentials, heat, light, and a piano. By choice they had no telephone, preferring a degree of isolation, and no running water, relying on a nearby spring and rainwater. The family spent time there every summer and many weekends and holidays throughout the year. Richter still spends her summers there, using it as her compositional retreat. About 90 percent of her works since 1970 have been started or come to fruition in this semi-isolated but spiritually inspiring location. (After Alan's death in 1988, the amenities were installed.)

Compositional "Postpartum Blues"

Reflecting back on this time in her life, Richter remarked on the letdown she often experienced following the elation from a performance or completion of a major work.

> Then came the ballet scores. I worked on those from about 1964 to '68, and when I finished, again there's that moment when it's like after you give birth, . . . did you have postpartum blues yourself? There's that sort of letdown, you know. . . . Whenever you have a big performance, and it's over, the next day it's so . . . I'd sit here and I'd feel so empty and I'd feel like crying. *[Laughs]*[20]

However, each time she experienced this anticlimax, something would come along to invigorate her again. She recalls:

> The very day (February 28, 1968) after I finished preparing the full score for *The Servant* and was basking in my freedom from that stressful task, the March 1 issue of *Life* magazine arrived in the mail and I read an article about Georgia O'Keeffe which included tiny little pictures of two of her paintings. I literally took one look at *Sky Above Clouds II* and was so inspired by its gentle floating quality that I immediately went to the piano and wrote the opening of what became my piano concerto *Landscapes of the Mind I*. The stark austerity of the second painting, *Pelvis 1*, generated inspiration for later sections in the piece. I thought the title of my concerto was my own invention, but in 1976, at the time of the premiere, I reread the *Life* magazine article and found that the author had written, "O'Keeffe's paintings could be considered landscapes of the mind."[21]

As the 1960s came to a close, Richter's children were becoming more independent and society was changing around her. Newly inspired, she began to explore much larger vistas for her musical creations.

4 Landscapes
1970s

"Do you think of yourself as a feminist?"

"No. Not actively. I don't think I have the problems that people who are active have. . . . You tell me: what do feminists really do for themselves?"

Marga Richter, interview
by Sharon Mirchandani, 2005

DURING THE 1970S Richter created some of her most important works: two large-scale orchestral scores, *Landscapes of the Mind I* and *Blackberry Vines and Winter Fruit*; two chamber music scores, *Landscapes of the Mind II* and *Landscapes of the Mind III*; and two significant piano pieces, *Remembrances* and *Requiem*, inspired by personal relationships. The music is her response to the beauty she found in nature, and intimacy.

Richter also became increasingly aware of the need to promote her own music. She recalls:

> In 1974 I began to understand that I needed to become more proactive in regard to furthering my career. To that end, I attended my first American Symphony Orchestra League convention, in Memphis, Tennessee, hoping to meet conductors who might program my music. As it turned out, I met a New York conductor, Michael Bartos, on the flight to Tennessee. We became friends, and he subsequently programmed my first piano concerto with me as soloist. The concert took place on January 31, 1975, at the Greenwich House Music School [New York]. Two scouts from the publisher of the work (Mills Music) attended with the intention of reporting back to Ainslee Cox, conductor of the Oklahoma Symphony, about whether I would be a viable soloist to present the work on a concert featuring American composer-pianists performing their own works, in January 1976, in Oklahoma, celebrating

> America's Bicentennial year. I passed the test and was engaged for the concert, which included Francis Thorne and Lee Hoiby.[1]

More prominent conductors became interested in Richter's orchestral works: Stanislaw Skrowaczewski (b. 1923) conducted *Lament* in 1976 with the Minnesota Orchestra and became a staunch supporter of her music.[2] That same year Gregory Millar conducted *Landscapes of the Mind I* with the Tucson Symphony Orchestra with William Masselos as soloist. And, Kenneth Schermerhorn conducted *Blackberry Vines and Winter Fruit* in 1977 with the Milwaukee Symphony Orchestra. Later, in 1989, conductor Harold Farberman recorded *Blackberry Vines and Winter Fruit* with the London Philharmonic Orchestra. Sheldon Morgenstern conducted *Lament* in 1977 with the Eastern Music Festival Orchestra in Greensboro, North Carolina, and in 1993 commissioned and conducted her triple concerto, also with the Eastern Music Festival Orchestra. One reason for this spate of performances was that the U.S. Bicentennial generated increased interest in programming U.S. composers. In addition, the backdrop to these performances and more was the second wave of feminism that had swept the nation.

Second-Wave Feminism

Although Richter has never referred to herself as a *feminist*, she is such an independent-minded person that she has led the life of "liberated woman" without thinking too much about it. During her childhood, her mother had been a strong role model, and her parents encouraged her to pursue not marriage but a career. This support for women having independent careers may be a hallmark of Richter's lineage: her mother's parents supported her choice of career, Richter and her husband enthusiastically sent daughter Maureen to India to further her sitar studies, and Maureen's daughter Stephanie dreams of opening an orphanage in Africa.

The kinds of obstacles Richter faced were not explicit, but rather matters like the social distance that separates women from men, and the role she fulfilled as primary caregiver to her children, even though her husband was supportive of her work. She feels in hindsight that it might have benefited her to sign her name as the genderless "M. Richter," since there was a definite, if unacknowledged, bias against women composers. "The very term tells the story. There is no category called 'men composers.'"[3]

In the early 1970s Richter began watching the soap opera *Days of Our Lives*. While many housewives watched soap operas while doing household chores, Richter recalls being hooked on it while engaged in the tedious process of writ-

10. Daughter Maureen with sitar, 1972.

ing out the full score of *Landscapes of the Mind I* and the piano reduction. She still watches *Days* today. The show is noted for its bold programming that addresses psychological problems and race issues. Its focus on human relationships and emotions appeal to Richter.

Teaching, a traditional goal for women, was never a goal of Richter's. Nevertheless, she did teach piano students since the age of fourteen and taught music appreciation at Nassau Community College on Long Island from 1971 to 1972. At first Richter found the college teaching to be fulfilling since she was given freedom to choose the music and ideas she wanted to present. After two semesters, though, the college standardized the curriculum and required her to teach from a specific text. She felt constrained by this and soon left college teaching.

In 1972, in keeping with her penchant for forming groups, Richter cofounded with Herbert Deutsch the Long Island Composers Alliance (LICA). As a cofounder, Richter led this organization through substantial growth, has served as codirector, president, and vice president, and remains an active member in her eighties. LICA continues to play an important role in new music sponsorship on Long Island, and in Queens, Brooklyn, and Manhattan, presenting some twenty concerts a year.

One front that feminism fights is against "ageism." Working women who are mothers have always been at a disadvantage professionally. Those with children have commonly had the greater responsibility of day-to-day child care than men, which takes time away from professional activities. They also have historically married younger than men and, in caring for their spouses and often their extended families, sacrificed some of their professional activities. Expanding their professional activities after their children are more independent, they may be considered too old for some opportunities. Richter experienced this when she applied in 1973 for a Rockefeller Foundation grant but was told that, at age forty-seven, she was past the cutoff age of forty-five. She viewed this as age discrimination.[4]

Though she herself always wanted to have children, Richter does not believe all women need to have children to feel "complete" and satisfied with their lives. However, she believes that if a woman has children, it may affect her career negatively, more so than it does for a man. Richter valued being a mother and took pride in it. In fact, she felt that motherhood contributed to her musical art by increasing her creative energy:

> I think they [the children] have added so much to me as a person. Having a full family life, and having the love and excitement of that has made my composing craft better than it would be if I had just looked in a book and written. I know of one piece that I wrote that is directly related to my son being in kindergarten.[5]

The piece she refers to is *Eight Pieces for Piano*, No. 5, which Richter wrote to express her anguish after leaving a wailing child on the first day of kindergarten.

Reflecting on her grown children leaving home during the 1970s, Richter continued:

> My career taking off now at the moment when they're taking off is so great. I always thought I would be lonely when they go. What am I going to do? I am going to be lonely, because I love them. They're so great to have around. But I'm also going to be able to write more, go places more, and get very involved. I don't want them to ever hear this and say: "Ahh, she can hardly wait until she can get us out of the house!" [But] I don't think they're ever going to feel that they can't get out of the house, that they shouldn't leave mommy or whatever and feel guilty or feel bad. They just better come and visit, that's all! *[Laughs]*[6]

These remarks show the exhilaration and satisfaction that Richter experienced from her professional life in addition to the joys of motherhood.

While Richter has never embraced the term *feminist*, she was involved in several activities catalyzed by the movement. Richter worked with composer Nancy Van de Vate to found the League of Women Composers in 1975.[7] Van de Vate served as chair until 1982, and Richter served on the first board of directors along with Radie Britain, Claire Polin, and Donna Robertson. Shortly thereafter, Pauline Oliveros joined the board. The organization's main objectives were to help women composers receive more commissions, performances, and recordings, and to fight for gender-blind and anonymous applications for composition awards. The organization became the International League of Women Composers in 1979. It eventually merged with the International Congress on Women in Music and the American Women Composers Inc. to become the International Alliance for Women in Music (IAWM). Today the IAWM runs an annual conference with concerts of music by women composers and publishes the *Journal of the International Alliance for Women in Music*.[8]

In 1977 Richter represented the League of Women Composers at the annual American Symphony Orchestra League convention in San Diego. Richter recalls beginning her address to the assemblage with "I would like to talk to you about sex," which elicited great laughter. This remark earned her personal approbation from none other than contemporary music's great wit, composer Morton Gould. Richter also organized a few concerts of music by women composers on behalf of the League of Women Composers (notably at the Museum of Modern Art in 1975), despite her uneasiness with separating music based on the gender of the composer.

Richter became a member of the American Women Composers around 1975. As part of this group, in 1979 between May 24 and June 3, along with composers Judith Lang Zaimont and Jeanne Singer, Richter codirected a "Six Day Panorama of Women's Music" at LaGuardia Community College. Numerous concerts, featuring personal appearances by eighteen American women composers, were presented including dramatic works, chamber music, orchestral works, electronic music, and choral music by both living and historical women composers. Included were her *Concerto for Piano and Violas, Cellos and Basses* (with her son Michael Skelly as soloist) and her *Soundings* for harpsichord (played by Sonia Gezairlian Grib).

During the 1970s Richter also became friends with violinist Marnie Hall because of their involvement in various women composers groups, concerts, and conferences. Hall had been a member of the all-women Vieuxtemps String Quartet and was asked on several occasions if the group performed any music by women composers. She began researching music by women, and eventually founded and became the recording producer for the nonprofit company Leonarda Productions. Leonarda's mission was to record and promote high-quality music by historical women composers, contemporary composers, and other overlooked composers regardless of gender. It was the only company committed to the recording of art music by women composers at the time and continues to be one of the few.

Leonarda disperses information on women composers and since the early 1980s has produced many of Richter's recordings.[9]

Marnie Hall describes Richter and their relationship:

> She's certainly a perfectionist, and her considerations are always artistic rather than commercial. I've made suggestions to her, such as writing shorter pieces and fanfares and more for winds and brass because they sell better than strings, even though I'm a string player, but she writes what pleases her. It's harder to get long pieces performed, but she writes what she wants to write, regardless, and doesn't seem to be swayed by commercial concerns. I admire that in people.
>
> Marga has always been present at our recording sessions, and it's both exhilarating and intense for both of us, since perfection is our goal, but is unachievable, and we're always working under a time constraint. We are both strong-willed and have strong opinions, and we're both difficult in such situations, but we admire each other and speak our minds, and we get along in the end, especially when a project has been completed.[10]

Hall also describes Richter's music:

> She often takes a theme and extends it using subtle harmonic changes that develop slowly over time giving the music a mesmerizing quality. You'll rarely find a rest in her music. Phrases flow seamlessly one into another. Her development is more an emotional buildup than a compositional technique.[11]

By 1979, Richter had given considerable thought to the effect of her gender on how her work was received. In a 1979 response to the question of differences between male and female composers, Richter wrote:

> It is fashionable, today, to say that there is *none*. But in private, the men mostly seem to feel that women's music is weaker, just as they feel *we* are weaker. For a long time I half believed that myself. Many of the early reviews of my music said things like—"it would seem impossible that this pungent and virile score could be the creation of a woman," or "women composers are rare birds, to be sure, but one with as dissonant and biting a style as Marga Richter's is decidedly a shock"—I took these as compliments.
>
> Today I feel quite differently. Not long ago, Karel Husa, a Pulitzer Prize winning composer, wrote to me after hearing several of my works covering a fifteen-year spread and said: "All of your works have the same qualities: gentleness, deep feeling, long phrasing, contrapuntally clear lines, all very sensitive qualities we do not hear too often, perhaps because they are feminine. I say this as a compliment, as I know these qualities from my home, having four daughters. By this I do not mean that force is not present. One hears it in the *Lament* as well as the piano-violin work."
>
> I take Mr. Husa's statement as a very real compliment, for I think he may have hit upon something. When we have enough music by women to make a study of the question, we may find that women are able to express emotion in a different way. I also feel it may turn

out that we construct music differently, when we are being ourselves and not following male models—not worse or better, just differently.

To put it simply, I now say, I don't think men can write music like women—nor vice versa. After all, I am a woman, I express what I am. Therefore it will be different from what a man will express—or any other woman.[12]

For Richter, music is an expression of an individual's identity and being a woman affects that identity.

During the 1980s, Richter did occasionally participate in concerts dedicated solely to women's music. In July 1986, a "Women in Music" symposium was organized by Barbara Harbach on the State University of Buffalo Amherst campus that featured a concert of chamber music by Joan Tower, a production of Vivian Fine's opera *The Women in the Garden*, and a concert of music presented by the New York Women Composers Inc. Three of Richter's piano works were performed on this last concert, her *Remembrances*, *Fragments*, and *Exequy*. The concert was reviewed by Thomas Putnam, who mulled over the term *woman composer*: "As a writer I find the term woman composer wordy. As a musician—I should say as a male musician—I find the term woman flutist exclusive, and perhaps (defense mechanism?) suggestive of a somewhat second-class executant." He praised Joan Tower's and Fine's works, but found only harsh words for the five works on the NYWC concert. About Richter's he wrote, "Marga Richter's three pieces for piano seem to be style studies, mild and forgettable."[13] Robert Friou, director of the NYWC and husband of composer Elizabeth Bell, wrote a letter of response to Putnam pointing out the "perception of a problem of systemic cultural discrimination against women in the field of musical composition; in particular in the genre of serious post-classical music." He defends the three piano works of Richter's and points out funding problems for larger works experienced disproportionately by women.[14]

Thirty years after the feminist movement began, Richter still longed for a society that no longer needed separate concerts for women composers. In 2005, when asked whether concerts by only women composers were necessary, Richter responded:

It probably isn't [necessary] . . . except I think it [the practice of programming more works by women] is backsliding. As soon as the economy's down, they don't hire the women. . . . and if you look at orchestra programs, you see mostly men these days.

Richter's continuation reveals her suspicion concerning the marketing of artists:

[The only women marketed are] a couple of high-profile women, and they're foreigners. That's another thing I don't like. If you come from Russia and you had a hard life, your music

> is [considered] better than someone's who comes from here and had a wonderful life, but still writes good music. They want the story with it. My life has been too good.[15]

Richter did express exasperation that women's music continues to be played less than men's music. She describes hearing the matter discussed by a radio broadcaster:

> he said, "Why, just last year we played a piece by Barbara Kolb." And I thought, "yes, just one time they played one woman and you're thinking that that's it . . . now we don't have to think about it anymore?" With all of the millions of men that they're playing? It was so fatuous. "Oh we've done that—look at that." I don't even like [the phrase] "women composers." . . . You know you don't ever say you went to a concert of men composers. You don't put out a record that says "music by men composers." Or "male composers." So if you're going to do a woman composer event, just do it, don't say it. Let people notice, "oh, they're all women." Instead of "come to the concert because they're women." . . . I guess that still interests some people, but I think as many people as it interests, it turns off the other half.[16]

Her comments reflect her steady belief that music should eventually stand on its own merits of beauty and expressiveness, rather than promotion due to social issues.

Growing Success

Nonetheless, the growth of support for women composers as a result of feminism helped create opportunities for success for Richter. Her music received performances and attention that had been difficult for women to achieve in the past, and the strength of her music withstood the scrutiny. Performances of her works received strong critical reviews, and she was interviewed frequently and earned numerous awards and grants.

These include an annual ASCAP Award since 1966, and over twenty grants from the "Meet the Composer" program sponsored by the New York State Council on the Arts through the 1970s and 1980s. Through the American Music Center, Richter received a copying grant from the Martha Baird Rockefeller Foundation to assist with the premiere of a major orchestral work, *Landscapes of the Mind I*. She also received grants from the National Endowment for the Arts to compose two other orchestral works, her *Music for Three Quintets and Orchestra* (later titled *Spectral Chimes/Enshrouded Hills*) (1980) and *Out of Shadows and Solitude* (1985).

Richter's first important radio interview was in 1974 when she was interviewed by Martin Bookspan for "The Composers Forum" broadcast on WNYC FM. Numerous radio interviews with Richter followed that were broadcast on various New York stations throughout the 1980s, including those by Andre Bernard, Tim Page, Jim Theobald, and David Soldier.

At Yale University in the 1960s, Vivian Perlis created the Oral History of American Music project in which extensive interviews with major figures in U.S. music and promising younger composers are recorded and preserved. The ongoing project currently contains about eight hundred interviews in its core section, including those with composers Nadia Boulanger, Aaron Copland, Harry Partch, Charles Seeger, William Schumann, John Cage, Lou Harrison, Jacob Druckman, Pauline Oliveros, and Ellen Taaffe Zwilich. In 1975 Richter was interviewed by Frances Harmeyer for the project.

Also in 1975, Richter received an important endorsement from the highly regarded publisher, Carl Fischer, when she was signed to an exclusive five-year publishing contract. The association with Carl Fischer has continued to this day on a nonexclusive basis.

In the fall of that year Richter received an exciting opportunity to have an all-Richter concert on September 5 and 6 in the Sculpture Garden of the Museum of Modern Art in New York as the opening of the Summergarden Composers Series. Performed on the concert were a selection of works composed between 1952 and 1965: *Soundings* for harpsichord (Leonard Raver), *Suite for Solo Viola* (Karen Phillips), *Ricercare* (Metropolitan Brass Quartet), *Eight Pieces for Piano* (Richter), *Variations on a Theme by Latimer* (four-hands), and *Melodrama* (for two pianos). The last two works were performed by Richter and Michael Skelly.

Acoustic difficulties at the concert were a problem. Allen Hughes reviewed the concert for the *New York Times*:

> Composers who write big brash works might have a chance in such a setting, but Miss Richter's music is characterized by refinement of detail, by counterpoints and dissonances worked out with care, by an economy that eliminates all but the essentials. Despite amplification, it was impossible to hear this music properly, to perceive the moods and sentiments it was intended to express. The pity is that Miss Richter deserves a decent hearing.[17]

The concert was also reviewed by Tom Johnson, and an illuminating exchange of letters between Johnson and Richter afterward again highlights the strong presence of serialism during this time and Richter's rejection of it. The first half of Johnson's lengthy review praises Richter's originality, variety of moods and textures, contrast and balance, understanding of instruments, tasteful expressiveness, refinement of allusion, rhythmic interest, and meticulous working out of material, for eleven paragraphs. He includes the comment, "She often works with interval patterns, showing that she is well aware of serial techniques, but she never exposes 12-tone rows in an obvious way." He ends this section with, "In short, her music is in very good taste." Johnson then continues with, "But whose

11. Marga Richter for Museum of Modern Art concert, ca. 1975.

good taste?" and philosophizes about the current state of music. "All those characteristics of her compositional style are attitudes which have been emphasized, and are generally still emphasized, in conservatory composition classes. . . . You can hear almost a fear of direct emotional expression. If you are so inclined, you can hear just plain snobbishness underlying all the good taste." The review was titled "Marga Richter: Good Taste Is Tuneless," and the caption under Richter's picture reads "Richter: 12-tone Snobbishness."[18]

Shortly after Richter read the review, she received a letter from Johnson apologizing for the way it was presented. He blamed a substitute editor for changing his original title, "The Good Taste of Marga Richter" saying "Tuneless" was somebody else's word, and "it sounds unnecessarily negative, aside from being completely irrelevant." He continued, "And I was dismayed when the picture caption summarized you as '12-tone snobbishness.' I only used the word 'snobbishness' once, of course, and then in a context which applied equally to me, Elliott Carter, Pierre Boulez, conservatory faculties—the whole shebang."[19]

Richter had indeed been offended by Johnson's review and defended herself in a reply, "I do *not* have a fear of direct emotional expression. In fact, I insist upon it, much to many persons' discomfort," describing examples of reactions to her music by performers, listeners and critics. In her correspondence to Johnson she also protests about

> being linked to the "establishment," Carter, Boulez, et al. Their work is anathema to me and I am constantly complaining that their intellectualized music *means* nothing. . . . You did not hear any obvious 12-tone rows in my music, not because I am so "tasteful" or excessively subtle, but because I find the whole serial business an absurdity which by some accident has produced a few good pieces. What I may know about interval patterns comes, not from the serialists, but from the same place where Schoenberg learned about them: Bach, Beethoven, etc.[20]

Her offer to meet and play some of her other music for Johnson was declined.

Reviewers of performances often called for more of Richter's music to be heard. For instance, Richter's *Lament* (1956) was played in 1976 by the Minnesota Orchestra in Minneapolis's Orchestra Hall. Critic Michael Anthony wrote: "The piece makes a striking effect on first hearing. . . . It is an early composition of Ms. Richter's and makes one eager to hear her more recent work.[21] And critic John Harvey wrote, "Now that the ice has been broken by this twenty year old work, perhaps it would not be amiss to suggest that we be given the chance to hear a product of the maturity of Richter's undeniable talent."[22] Indeed those opportunities arose, with nearly all of Richter's music receiving performances, many of them repeatedly through the years. Most notable are the performances of Richter's orchestral works, as these are more difficult performances to procure.

Landscapes Series

Throughout the 1970s, Richter worked on her *Landscapes of the Mind* series. This series consists of three separate works for different forces: a concerto for piano with orchestra, a work for violin and piano, and a piano trio. While each of the three works is unique, all three share some musical material as well. Richter wrote about her *Landscape* series:

> All three pieces seek to convey the spaciousness and spare serenity of the paintings contrasted with inner turbulence, urgency and ultimate isolation (although the concerto ends with a triumphant Raga section).[23]

The paintings to which she refers are two by Georgia O'Keeffe, *Sky Above Clouds II* and *Pelvis I* that Richter had first seen in a 1968 issue of *Life* magazine (see chapter 3). These prompted her to begin *Landscapes of the Mind I.*

LANDSCAPES OF THE MIND I (PIANO CONCERTO NO. 2) (1974)

Richter has suggested that the softness of the clouds contrasting with the hardness of bone could be thought of as analogous to traditional female and male qualities, but mostly she has stressed that she was trying to capture the beauty of the paintings.[24] Richter was often inspired by strong women artists (Virginia Woolf, Emily Dickinson, Eileen O'Leary, Sara Teasdale, Gabriela Mistral, and Anne Lindbergh) and, in this case, was drawn to O'Keeffe's strength, her monumentality, and her otherworldliness. O'Keeffe had broken away from the miniatures, portraits, domestic scenes, and images of women and children that had been more typical of women painters. Instead she painted flowers, rocks, shells, animal bones, and landscapes with vivid, powerful colors. It was these paintings of landscapes and bones that inspired Richter.

Landscapes of the Mind I is in two very distinct parts, played without pause. The score is for full orchestra (minus trombones and tuba) supplemented with electric guitar, electric bass guitar, amplified tamboura, marimba, celesta, harp, tom-tom, and "Indian drum" (tabla). Richter's work shares some surface features with Charles Ives's Fourth Symphony, which is also about thirty minutes long, has a large orchestra, and has a quasi-spiritual mood. Richter wrote in a program note:

> The piece is not written according to any "system," but might be called "transcendental expressionism." It is neither tonal nor atonal, but has definite feelings of tone-centers, especially in the second-section Raga where the tone "C" is repeated continually, except for a brief surcease in the piano cadenza near the end of the piece.[25]

The opening of the concerto suggests the floating, nebulous image of *Sky Above Clouds II*, with a soft upward arpeggio, in piano alone, spanning five octaves and ushering in a tenuous, highly chromatic melodic motive supported by an exotic, otherworldly orchestral accompaniment. Though they are gentle in dynamic, the harmonies in the first section are unresolved and quite dissonant, consisting of augmented octaves, major sevenths, and perfect fourths interlocked with tri-tones. The ethereal mood is sustained for fifty-nine measures until shattered by a sudden sharply percussive and dissonant intrusion that develops into a free-for-all in which many layers of music struggle to exist coequally. This is followed by another contemplative section, where the piano and orchestra have their own meters and material: piano in $\frac{4}{4}$, molto rubato; orchestra in $\frac{3}{4}$, in strict time. They eventually come together and reach a reprise of the opening themes, gradually reaching a shattering climax and then subsiding to a quiet transition to the raga section.

The decision to write a raga for the second part of the concerto was made almost immediately after the first few bars of the piece were written. Richter recalls how she was first exposed to Indian music:

> I first heard Indian classical music, a recording by sitarist Ravi Shankar, in 1967, while visiting Lenore Engdahl in Wellesley [Mass.]. I immediately knew I wanted to write a piano piece that would express both the serenity and the raw ecstasy of this kind of musical expression. As my concerto progressed I had an "aha" moment when I knew that this piece was the place for my "raga."[26]

Richter was primarily interested in Indian music as source material for her composition, saying,

> I did not want to try to write authentic Indian music. . . . What I wanted to do was to transfer the melodic and rhythmic beauty and intensity of that kind of musical experience to Western instruments, using my own compositional techniques.[27]

She selected the prominent Hindu raga "Marwa" that uses only the notes in the following scale: C D♭ E F♯ A B C, and is notable for omitting the fifth of the scale. What appealed to her was the inherent dissonance between the D♭ and the C♮ tonic, which is used as a continuous drone throughout this section.[28] (She also enjoyed the similarity between its name and hers.)

For the transition between the two sections of the concerto, Richter drew on her extensive exposure to the music of Bob Dylan, due to her daughter's obsession with it (and him), on the family's seven-week camping trip to the West Coast and back by VW bus, in 1969. Dylan's records were played incessantly in the bus on a tiny portable record player. Richter was hooked. (Through her children, she also came to love the music of the Beatles, Creedence Clearwater Revival, Chicago, Simon and Garfunkel, and James Taylor, whose version of "You've Got a Friend" had particular resonance for her.)

> Dylan's *Sad-Eyed Lady of the Low-Lands* was a particular favorite of mine, mysterious, touching, ambiguous. When the time came to transition to the raga, the refrain from that song just kind of inserted itself as a simple melodic phrase, marked "very slow," to tie the two sections of the concerto together. I changed the key from major to minor, altered the rhythm and enveloped it in ascending, predominantly major-seventh, arpeggiated figures. The proof of my successful camouflage came when I proudly played the passage for Michael and Maureen (assuming they would make the connection), saying, "Listen to what I put into my piece today," and received only blank stares.[29]

Two additional arpeggios usher in the raga, helping to unify the two sections. The second arpeggio uses only notes from the raga scale, selected because they match the dissonant character of the preceding arpeggio of the first section.

Throughout the second section, descending minor thirds in the raga from C to A, A to F♯, and E to C♯ create a link to the descending third prominent in the first section's melodic line. This transition moves satisfyingly from a high incidence of chromaticism to the largely diatonic framework of the raga.

The slow unfolding of the Marwa raga over the C drone (in both piano and orchestra) creates a hypnotic effect. Throughout its ten-minute duration it undergoes countless metric displacements and rhythmic expansions, from half notes to quarters to eighths to sixteenths to thirty-seconds to triplet thirty-seconds. Above this drone, the raga is by turns otherworldly, energetic, tender, melancholy, soothing, or violent. The work ends fortissimo with the soloist furiously playing syncopated percussive C♯ octaves in the right hand against left-hand thirty-second-note arpeggiated figures. Against this, the orchestra contributes a blaze of percussion and a triumphant descending statement of the raga scale.

When she finished the concerto, Richter sent Georgia O'Keeffe a long letter telling her about the work's genesis and offering to send her a tape if a premiere took place. She also asked if a tape of *Landscapes of the Mind II* for violin and piano would interest her. O'Keeffe's succinct but gracious reply is one of Richter's treasures:

> Dear Ms. Richter: Thank you for your kind letter and brochure. I will be pleased to get the tapes of your music.
>
> Very sincerely, [signed "Georgia O'Keeffe"][30]

Richter sent the tape of *Landscapes II* to O'Keeffe, but there was no reply. Richter posits five reasons: O'Keeffe did not receive it; she did not listen to it; she did not like it; she did not think a reply was necessary; the tape was blank. The last reason was a possibility because a tape made at the same time, sent to a conductor, turned out to have nothing on it. After the *Landscapes I* premiere, Richter did not send a tape of the performance to O'Keeffe, a decision she came to regret.

Landscapes of the Mind I received its premiere with the Tucson Symphony conducted by Gregory Millar on March 19, 1976.[31] William Masselos was the pianist. A number of favorable reviews followed. Critic Lawrence W. Cheek wrote a review for the *Tucson Daily Citizen* titled "Symphony's 'Landscapes' a Real Triumph":

> The title really suggests the essence of the work. [It] seems like a succession of craggy, smoldering mental images malignantly parading past like figures on a Hellenic frieze.
>
> The shorter second section is built around a single droning note, in the style of an Indian raga. To me, it seemed less successful: There are severe limits to the harmony and range of expression a composer can manage when at least one tone is frozen throughout an entire movement. . . .

> In contrast to the allergic welcome Tucson audiences usually give to progressive new music, *Landscapes* had a fairly decent reception last night at the Music Hall. Miss Richter, in town for the premiere, was called up to the stage and was applauded warmly.[32]

Ken LaFave reviewed the performance for the *Arizona Daily Star*, noting Richter's gender:

> Potent and assertive—anything but true to the stereotyped concepts of how music by a woman should sound. . . . Happily, last night's audience seemed aware of the fact that *Landscapes* is a work of vital musical ideas which have been woven into a solid piece of tonal architecture. They might not have put it that way, and many audience members were openly puzzled about their reactions, but the sense of something important going on was in general attendance.
>
> Ms. Richter is a patient composer. Her ideas happen naturally, and she is content to develop them in a way that does not hurry or deform their organic growth. *Landscapes I* is in two parts, the first part of which contains a great deal of adrenalin-forcing rhythmic invention, which Masselos and a feverish Tucson Symphony Orchestra brought off with flair.
>
> The second section was conceived as a raga, but in the western context it comes off more like a prolonged recitative over a pedal "C." Richter does about everything possible within that limited framework—the final measures are especially powerful—but the constant drone of the "C" comes dangerously close to maddening at times.
>
> Her massive pile-ups of sound are experienced not so much as static dissonance, but as layers of sound, each layer being self-containedly consonant.
>
> It is hoped that *Landscapes* will enjoy repeated performances—it deserves them.[33]

Reviewer James Uhrig thought the audience was not responsive enough to the work:

> The orchestra seemed to have great difficulty keeping count, but made a brave effort to sound the right notes at the right time. . . . At the end of the piece the audience applauded, and conductor, composer and soloist took their well-earned bows; but there just wasn't sufficient enthusiasm for that applause to last more than two bows apiece. It is a pity that this work should be unveiled before a largely unresponsive public.[34]

Robert L. Cherry also reviewed the work at length for *Tucson Tonight* and *High Fidelity/Musical America*. In the latter, Cherry concludes:

> This concerto, a well-crafted blend of realism and transcendentalism, and of East and West, is unconventional but not eccentric, occasionally dissonant but never offensive, individualistic and original but not avant-garde. It is a complex but uncomplicated psychomusical experience that is immediately accessible, emotionally appealing, and has an uncanny amount of common sense.[35]

Despite these largely favorable reviews, *Landscapes of the Mind I* was not performed again until Natalie Hinderas and the Atlanta Symphony Orchestra with

Louis Lane conducting played it in March 1986 with the composer present.[36] This concert was in conjunction with the Fourth International Congress on Women in Music, and Mary Brown Hinely wrote about the event, "This concert was a significant fulfillment of dreams and efforts to mainstream women's music."[37]

Critic Derrick Henry interviewed Richter prior to the concert. In the interview Richter says she never considered herself a "woman composer" but concedes "it is possible there was a time not too long ago when women's music was not considered for performances. Around 1974 the women's movement helped bring our music to public attention; the bicentennial year benefited *all* American composers, men and women. I'm not totally sure that there are *no* differences between the music of women and men. Perhaps we simply lack the perspective to see these differences."[38]

After the Atlanta concert Henry also wrote a lengthy review of the work that opened with "It is an extraordinary piece. It is also extraordinarily difficult. . . . Over its 30-minute length, the piece challenges, compels, stimulates and ultimately enthralls." Henry goes on to compare the work's style to minimalism:

> In some respects, Ms. Richter's hypnotic repetition of short motives is typical of the latest Western musical vogue, "minimalism," which in itself is influenced by Eastern music. But her musical language is far more complex than that of such prominent practitioners of minimalism as Philip Glass and Steve Reich.
>
> The textures are richer. The rhythms are more intricate. Traditional chord progressions are virtually non-existent. And while Ms. Richter's music develops slowly (the first big climax does not come until nearly 20 minutes into the score), it is not static. Material introduced in a simple, quiescent manner subtly grows until it eventually explodes into a cataclysm of confusion.

Henry concludes with strong praise:

> *Landscapes* is a layered work, with different levels piled on top of one another. The piano part was actually written separately from the rest of the score, and could function as an independent entity. It is the interaction of these often contradictory layers that gives the piece its palpable energy and tension.
>
> In short, it is a work worth hearing. And worth recording. Indeed, a carefully produced recording of this superb performance would better serve our orchestra and the musical public than all those unadventurous albums for which the ASO recently received Grammy nominations and awards.[39]

Landscapes of the Mind I was Richter's largest and most ambitious work to date and became a source of inspiration in terms of textures and scale for subsequent works such as *Blackberry Vines and Winter Fruit* (1976), *Spectral Chimes/Enshrouded Hills* (1980), and *Out of Shadows and Solitude* (1985).

LANDSCAPES OF THE MIND II FOR VIOLIN AND PIANO (1971)

The *Landscapes* series continued with the fifteen-minute *Landscapes of the Mind II* for violin and piano (1971), written for Daniel Heifetz.

In a letter to Heifetz, Richter wrote passionately about the exuberance she felt having completed the work and gave him some romantic suggestions for imagery:

> Oct. 13, 1971
> Dear Danny,
>
> A great feeling of joy is beginning to well up within me. Your music is on the way to you, and I can begin to relax. It has been a tremendous struggle, for eight months. Now I am finished, and, hopefully, you can begin.
>
> We miss you. Maureen and I had a very special feeling for you from the very beginning, and I think you reciprocate. I hope you come back to New York, soon. I'm going to try to get you to play in Huntington again, maybe with the symphony Seymour Lipkin conducts (a Curtis-type!)
>
> About the music.
>
> I have an uneasy feeling that you are not yet quite sure whether you can make it a piece you really *love*. *I* know that you can, but *you* don't. Am I wrong?
>
> To me, this music is other-worldly, ethereal, symbolic, but always infused with feeling, meaning, passion—Can you understand the combination? If you let each chromatic upward turn grow from the last one and arrive at the peak and return, all on one tenuous thread, all on one deep and slightly agonized breath, you will begin to find your way.
>
> You are young, but you have experienced much already. Draw on that, try to find the mood you understand when high in the mountains or contemplating the sea, and the world beyond the concrete. That feeling of sudden emptiness, followed by knowledge of the sublime, followed by angry denial of forces producing pain, followed by inner visions of the ultimate beauty of the universe.
>
> Followed by lots of hard work!
>
> Just before you begin to play, you must leave the world as it is, wood, strings, flesh, distractions, and enter the world you are about to create—a visionary world of light and darkness, pain and pleasure, weightless, beautiful, remote and immediate.
>
> Please, please write and let us know how and what you are doing. When I can get my piano tuned and repaired, I will tape the piano part.
>
> Meanwhile, on Monday I begin the orchestration of the piano concerto, put off for a whole year!—Talk about struggle. I hope I have the strength!
>
> Much love—Marga[40]

Sometimes, as here, Richter felt that a work might not be what the performer was expecting but thought that, if the performers would give it enough serious consideration, they would come to truly appreciate the work. As Heifetz did not play the work right away, Richter premiered it herself with violinist Jo Margaret Farris in Coe Hall, Oyster Bay, on Long Island. The work was also performed by Jerilyn Jorgensen, violin, and Martin Amlin, piano, for an American Society of University Composers 1975 Region 2 concert at Eastman School of Music in Rochester, New York.

Eventually Heifetz did play the New York City premiere of *Landscapes of the Mind II* in Alice Tully Hall, on April 26, 1977. Richter attended a rehearsal of the piece a few days before this concert, at which time Heifetz informed her that in his "out-of-town" performances of the work he had cut a sizable number of bars from the beginning of the piece because he thought it should move along more quickly. In her words:

> I was astounded, and strenuously defended the integrity of the piece. He did not capitulate. Overnight I decided to tell him to play it as written or not at all. I was willing to sacrifice the New York premiere. Before I had a chance to call him in the morning, he called me and graciously said he would play it as written.[41]

Of the concert, *New York Times* critic Allen Hughes wrote:

> Miss Richter's piece . . . is written in such a way that it responded to Mr. Heifetz' way of playing, and it made a favorable impression on this listener. . . . The contrasts of energy and mood are handled adroitly and hold the interest for the twelve minutes or so that the piece lasts.[42]

The work received numerous positive reviews and a mention in *The Literature of Chamber Music*, where Arthur Cohn wrote "the evidence signifies a lasting contribution to violin-piano literature." Robert Jones of the *New York Daily News* described it as "a marvelously, moody, impressionistic work." *Chicago Tribune* critic John Von Rhein wrote, "none of the unviolinistic effects of which many contemporary composers are fond. Throughout there is a certain haunted quality." And Harris Goldsmith of *High Fidelity/Musical America* called it "one of the most attractive contemporary pieces I have heard in a long time."[43] Heifetz went on to play *Landscapes of the Mind II* in his prize-winning program for the 1978 Sixth International Tchaikovsky Competition and on tour in the Soviet Union and the United States. *Landscapes of the Mind II* was also included in the repertory list for the Kennedy Center–Rockefeller Foundation International Competition for the Performance of American Music, 1980 Violin Competition.

Richter wrote a detailed unpublished typescript of her analysis of *Landscapes of the Mind II* in which she describes the opening of both *Landscapes I* and *Landscapes II* as reflecting "the spacious, floating atmosphere of the O'Keeffe paintings." She then describes the solo piano beginning of *Landscapes II* as "a conscious resolution of *Landscapes of the Mind I*."[44] *Landscapes of the Mind II* uses the three basic melodic figures from *Landscapes of the Mind I*: the widely spaced arpeggio figure of augmented octaves and major sevenths, the tritone plus superimposed perfect fourth chord, and melodic material in seconds that features a minor third (or augmented second).

Despite these recognizable similarities to *Landscapes of the Mind I*, *Landscapes of the Mind II* is not simply a transcription. The Indian raga and drone are not present at all, and there is a much greater emphasis on the descending minor third as a melodic element. The tri-tone combined with perfect fourth is also used more extensively as an ostinato in the bass in various rhythmic patterns. *Landscapes of the Mind II* is freer in form with many small contrasting sections that are in turn poignant, turbulent, restrained, wild, waltzlike, lyrical, and exuberant. The work ends quietly rather than with the flourish and bombast of *Landscapes of the Mind I*.

LANDSCAPES OF THE MIND III FOR PIANO, VIOLIN, AND CELLO (1978)

In 1978 Richter received a commission from the National Federation of Music Clubs for a work to be premiered at their 40th Biennial Convention in Portland, Oregon. For this, she composed her *Landscapes of the Mind III* for piano, violin, and cello (1978). Pianist Katherine George, violinist Kathryn Grey, and cellist India Zerbe premiered the work on April 29, 1979.

While, again, some of the material is related to *Landscapes of the Mind I*, this piece is more introverted than the earlier two, and Richter once reflected that the piece expressed some of her sadness at her daughter's departure from home for an extended sojourn in India to study sitar.[45] She wrote in a program note:

> Landscapes III, even more than the other two, *sustains* the floating, spare, *internal* feelings engendered by the paintings (especially "Sky above Clouds"). It begins quietly but with coiled intensity, explodes early on and then becomes more and more contemplative, its moments of turmoil spaced further and further apart. It ends softly and ambiguously, with a questioning finality.[46]

The work's premiere received a favorable review by Heuwell Tircuit in the *San Francisco Chronicle*: "The Richter is a humdinger piece, lyrical and nostalgic but up to the minute in style."[47] Of a Huntington performance, Bob Micklin wrote in *Newsday* that Richter's third *Landscapes* had "a reflective, rather hypnotic feeling."[48] In addition to many performances on Long Island from 1979 to 2008, the piece was performed at the Longy School in Cambridge, Massachusetts, on October 26, 1979, and the Fontana Festival in Kalamazoo, Michigan, on August 3, 1988.

Shorter Works

In addition to the *Landscapes* series, Richter composed a number of smaller works at this time, including *Four Piano Pieces* (1970), *Country Auction* for band (1976), and *Variations on a Theme by Neithart Von Reuenthal* for organ (1974).

Richter wrote well-received entertaining and educational works for children and collected a set of her intermediate teaching pieces to use with her own piano students as *Four Piano Pieces*. The titles are "Hugh's Piece," "Elephants and Violets," "For Something That Had Gone Before," and "Bits and Snatches." These engaging works teach children twentieth-century harmonies and techniques such as forearm glissandos, playing with the fists, slapping on the wood under the keyboard, or tapping on the piano lid. "Bits and Snatches" requires a small metal drum for some right-hand parts with the left hand always on the piano. Richter also composed *Short Prelude in Baroque Style* (1974) at this time for her friend Barbara Kupferberg to play on her clavichord.

Richter's *Country Auction* for band (1976) was commissioned by Carl Fischer for a project to generate pieces at an appropriate technical level for school bands. Richter was the only female composer included in the project. The other composers Fischer engaged were Ulysses Kay, Warren Benson, Elie Siegmeister, Henry Brant, Leo Smit, Samuel Adler, Howard Hanson, and Carlos Chávez.[49] In this delightful piece, Richter captures the spirit of an auction by having an "auctioneer" start the piece, calling out an invitation for bids on an item, such as a real lamp, and shouting, "All right, the lamp. What am I bid for it?" The band's rhythms then correspond to bids of various amounts of money. In Richter's words,

> This piece was inspired by a real auctioneer in Vermont (Bus Mars, of Pawlet, whose auctions were attended as much for entertainment as for buying or selling, and to whom this piece is dedicated), and uses his rhythms and sense of humor. When the bidding reached a feverish pitch between two people and suddenly one of them dropped out he would shout, "Well, it's your turn!"[50]

Richter incorporated this moment in her piece by having a designated group of players jump up and holler those words at another group, which responds with a well-aimed blast of music at them. The piece ends in a fortissimo riot of sound.

A more serious work, *Variations on a Theme by Neithart Von Reuenthal* was commissioned by and dedicated to organist Thomas E. Garbrick. Von Reuenthal was a minnesinger from the Middle Ages. Richter presents his thirty-two-measure song, in Dorian mode, "Winter Wie Ist Nu Dein Kraft," monophonically and then offers thirteen colorful variations on it ranging from eleven to forty-eight measures in length, in a variety of meters. From the fifth variation on, the variations become increasingly chromatic and complex until the eleventh variation, for pedals alone, which is totally diatonic, and serves as a brief respite before the climactic twelfth one. In the twelfth variation, also fortissimo, the original theme is reprised in the pedals below a startlingly dissonant chromatic harmonization of the hymn *Abide with Me*, ending triple-forte on a chord of eight pitches, including the pedal D. The final variation closes the work softly with a sustained tonic pedal throughout and the original melody reprised with a gently chromatic descant above.

Organist Leonard Raver premiered *Variations on a Theme by Neithart von Reuenthal* on a concert of works by contemporary American composers on July 9 and 10, 1976, in the Museum of Modern Art's Summergarden series. Critic Byron Belt wrote in his review of the performance, "As Miss Richter's *Variations* moved further from the theme itself, the work grew into rich development of sounds that made splendid use of the organ's tonal potentials."[51] Richter was the only female composer on the program, which included works by Vincent Persichetti, Samuel Barber, Myron Roberts, Gerald Busby, and Elliott Schwartz. Among other performers of *Variations* are organists Julie Collins, Adel Heinrich, Carson Cooman, and Robert Ludwig.

A Touch of American Transcendentalism

During the fall and winter of 1975–76, Richter composed her thirteen-minute symphonic poem *Blackberry Vines and Winter Fruit*. The work was commissioned by conductor Louis Calabro and the Sage City Symphony, a semiprofessional orchestra in North Bennington, Vermont, and premiered by them on October 17, 1976. (At the end of the concert, the audience was invited to dance to Strauss waltzes.) It is scored for: 3 flutes (2nd doubling on alto flute, 3rd doubling on piccolo), 2 oboes, 2 clarinets (2nd doubling on bass clarinet), 2 bassoons; 4 horns in F, 3 trumpets in B♭, 2 trombones, 1 tuba; timpani, percussion (celesta, vibraphone, tenor drum, tom-tom, bass drum, cowbell, small gong, maracas); harp, and strings.

Richter describes *Blackberry Vines and Winter Fruit* as "an attempt to portray in music the feelings engendered by the lonely beauty of a winter landscape." While searching for a title that would be descriptive of these feelings, she came across a book by photographer Eliot Porter titled *In Wildness Is the Preservation of the World*. Porter's book juxtaposes his own nature photographs with selections from Thoreau's *Journal* and *Walden*. Like Thoreau's *Journal*, Porter's presentation is organized by the season.

David Brower, in his forward to Porter's book, characterizes Porter's photographs as music:

None but a very literal person would fail to see that color is his music, that there is melody line, counterpoint, harmony, dynamics, voicing, and phrasing all there for those who will listen.

There is absolute pitch, too—absolute color pitch. . . . If we are very fortunate, once in a while they may perform for us the quiet symphony that responds to his baton.[52]

Richter created her title from the Thoreau quotations accompanying two of Porter's photos. The first is of a yellow-brown field with reddish-brown vines amid the grasses, juxtaposed with the line: "blackberry vines here and therein sunny places look like a streak of blood on the grass."[53] The second photo is of a yellow, dried-out winter field with reddish brown twigs and a contrasting tree with white bark. It is accompanied with the text: "The flower falls in spring or summer, the fruit and leaves fall or wither in autumn, but the blushing twigs retain their color throughout. . . . They are winter fruit."[54] Both photos show the dull reddish-brown color within the bleak, dry winter fields, rather than the green grasses, flowers, ponds, or wild animals in the other photos.

The Milwaukee Symphony conducted by Kenneth Schermerhorn performed the work on March 19 and 20, 1977. Reviewer Lawrence B. Johnson questioned and then strengthened the connection between Richter's work and Thoreau's lines with this description of the music:

even if one tastes more of fruit than of winter, even if Miss Richter might as usefully entitled it *Essay for Orchestra, Blackberry Vines* is not unappealing music. It sprouts simply, with an ostinato runner that issues from two flutes and piccolo and progressively intertwines itself into dense foliage teeming with instrumental color and rhythmic life. From the engrossing complexity and dramatic pitch of this middle section, in which the ostinato figure takes on many new appearances, all tension is suddenly thrown off and the music begins a long fall through reiterated patterns in the strings. In a formal process akin to chaconne, the strings' continuous weaving becomes the backdrop for an imaginative play of brasses and woodwinds—now bold and dominant, now mere innuendoes—until the work melts quietly away.[55]

The work consists of four closely related sections. The music becomes, very gradually, faster and louder, starting pianissimo (*pp*) and very slowly, and climaxing at fortissississimo (*ffff*) toward the end of the fourth section. Groups of instruments are each assigned an ostinato line with its own rhythmic value, thereby creating layers of quarters, sixteenths, triplets, and nontuplets. The work then subsides dynamically and rhythmically. Richter describes the four sections:

The first section opens with a piccolo and two flutes obsessively repeating a melodic motif which permeates the whole piece: a rising minor second followed by a falling major second. The intervals gradually expand in a pattern that parallels the way that a tree grows and finally comes to rest on a sustained minor ninth.

At this point the violins emerge to begin the second section in which the original motif, slightly altered, is repeated many times and surrounded by rapid, swirling figures. The section ends with a statement in the horns. This occurs simultaneously with the beginning of the multi-layered third section in which a Gregorian-chant-like melody floats over the top, pitted against a recurring melodic ostinato in ever-changing orchestral colors, accompanied by a rhythmic ostinato in the percussion section, and irregularly assaulted by a high, penetrating, descending motif designed to imitate the unearthly sound of the sarangi (a bowed string instrument of India). These sarangi utterances are always preceded by rapid ascending passages suggestive of the continuous growth and movement in nature.

The complexities of section three give way to a simple five-note statement in the strings. Clusters of tones in the cellos emerge, suggesting clumps of tangled vines breaking through the snow. An oboe solo introduces an expanded version of the opening motif of the piece. This theme, or variants of it, is gradually taken up by other wind and brass instruments in more and more rapid tempos. It culminates in a canonic statement by two trumpets which occurs just after a passage in the low brass which seems a natural outgrowth of the basic material of the piece, although it is in fact a direct quote from Bach's *B Minor Mass*.

After this climax, the music quickly subsides. A final statement of the theme is heard in the oboe; the flute plays a ghostly reminder of the Gregorian melody; and there is a whisper of the first notes of the oboe theme by the horn, supported by harp and solo double bass two and a half octave below—a streak of blood on the grass, set off against the winter fruit.[56]

In addition to the inspiration from the Thoreau lines, the subtly changing tone colors of the work and its emphasis on variants of the opening theme may reflect something of American Transcendentalism's belief in underlying meanings.

On April 25 and 26, 1978, Calvin Simmons (substituting for the regular conductor, Harold Farberman, who chose the piece) conducted the work with the Oakland Symphony in California. This performance drew some harsh reviews. In a review that also describes the substitute conductor as "inconsistent" and the solo pianist for another piece as "not at all confident," Michael Walsh wrote:

Marga Richter's *Blackberry Vines and Winter Fruit*, a tedious attempt to substitute atmosphere for musical substance, opened the concert. One would have thought that this quintessentially '60s aesthetic had been long since discredited, but, amazingly, *Blackberry Vines* is a work of 1976. However, it does offer young composers a textbook example of how not to employ the ostinato principle, using it as an end in itself, rather than as a dramatic gesture underlining a musical point.[57]

Robert Commanday wrote:

The title . . . is more interesting than the piece, which intends to evoke images of a wintry scene. The fact that it didn't for me is less important than the weak compositional craft that kept it from holding the attention on purely musical terms.[58]

In a more neutral review, Paul Hertelendy wrote only that

> Richter's wafting *Blackberry Vines and Winter Fruit* proved to be a post-Ives programmatic piece with extensive overlays and even a bit of microtonality.[59]

Since there is no microtonality in the score, perhaps what was heard was the result of out-of-tune playing in the strings and insufficient rehearsal time and commitment to the piece.

Despite the two negative reviews, the work continued to attract attention.

Following a performance on February 3, 1981, by the Juilliard Philharmonia conducted by José Serebrier for the Juilliard Festival of Contemporary Music, the *New York Times* reviewer Allen Hughes wrote:

> The general mood in this instance is one of vague pessimism, perhaps futility. Nevertheless, there is quite a bit of beauty in the music. The materials and textures (some repeated frequently) are often reminiscent of Ives. . . . In any case, there is something authentic and moving about Richter's moody score.[60]

After an April 25, 1986, performance in Williamstown, Massachusetts, by the Berkshire Symphony conducted by Julius Hegyi, another reviewer compares the work to impressionism and also comments on the repetition:

> It has a pervading wailing quality, underscored by reiterated dissonances and a lengthy, descending ostinato. The work is reminiscent of impressionism in a new language. Although well-played, it was too repetitive to hold the listener's interest.[61]

In 1990 the work was released on a CD performed by the London Philharmonic Orchestra conducted by Harold Farberman. This CD was selected as one of five significant new releases for "The Want List 1991" in *Fanfare* by staff reviewer Stephen Ellis, who called *Blackberry Vines and Winter Fruit* "a vital portrayal."[62] An engraved edition of the score was published by Carl Fischer Inc. in 1978.

Piano Works

Remembrances was written in 1977 for the seventh anniversary broadcast of *The Listening Room* on New York's WQXR radio station, hosted by Robert Sherman, to whom it is dedicated. The work was begun as a piece for piano four-hands to be played by Sherman and his mother, the eminent Nadia Reisenberg. It soon became apparent that only two hands were needed, and when Sherman demurred, citing "stage fright" he asked Richter to do the honors, which she did. The program aired, live, on January 4, 1978. Richter used variants of the opening theme song for *The Listening Room*, from Jacques Ibert's *Divertissement* as a tribute to the program.

Richter includes detailed performance notes, as she does in many of her scores, to help guide the performer, and Bob Doerschuk listed *Remembrances* as a recommended keyboard work in *Contemporary Keyboard*, describing it as

> an 82-bar delicacy . . . a well-balanced blend of soft dissonance and floating melody, set in $\frac{3}{4}$, except for an occasional measure of $\frac{4}{4}$ that adds a slight breadth to the waltz feel. There are no difficulties or fireworks; instead, an ascending eighth-note motif, running up a modified diminished arpeggio, appears repeatedly in the midst of the ostinato figure that evolves and transforms itself in the left hand.[63]

Mostly homophonic with arpeggiated chords in the left hand, many of the harmonies are diminished or minor triads in second inversion, and tri-tones interlocked with perfect fourths. Some trills and septuplet figures in the upper register give it an ethereal quality.

In 1978 Richter began to write a piece requested by guitarist Jerry Willard. Richter wrote about the work's maturity:

> *Requiem* was begun as a piece for solo guitar. When it eventually became apparent that it needed more power and sonority than one guitar could provide, it became a work for solo piano. However, the original conception is cogently evident in the many guitar-like passages and the circumscribed four-and-a-third-octave range. It was written in response to a deeply felt personal loss, and became a plea for the ultimate repose of all departed souls.[64]

The twenty-one-minute *Requiem* does contain many aspects of guitar style with the melodic line woven into broken chords. In form, *Requiem* is rondolike with a pattern of ABCBA'DA".[65] Ostinatos, chromaticism, and varying textures generate the sections, and the C section is especially exhilarating, with dynamic chords alternating between the hands. Maurice Hinson describes *Requiem* as "evocative, intense writing, long pedals, enormously effective. D[ifficult]."[66]

Pianist Sorrel Hays (formerly Doris Hays) champions Richter's *Requiem*, frequently performing it in recitals throughout Germany and the United States:

> I like the piece very much, for its intransigent and unrelenting perusal of the theme. Since I am a composer as well as pianist, I have usually only chosen to perform other composer works which have something that grabs me, either structurally or harmonically. Marga's structural sense is fascinating.[67]

In the same communication, Hays also describes a portrait of Richter painted by Roberta Reichbach in 1984:

> It is large and vivid and Marga did not like it at first, but I think came to like it later. Very strong painting and a very strong portrait of Marga's uncompromising self.[68]

Requiem has received numerous performances and reviews over the years. Byron Belt wrote an unenthusiastic review in 1979: "Marga Richter presented her moving, moody and over-long *Requiem*. The pianist offered a compelling performance, but the thundering chordal sections seemed somehow empty compared to the more meandering lyrical portions."[69] However, in a review of Hays's 1981 Spoleto performance, critic Allan Kozinn wrote, "The most satisfying work on the program was Marga Richter's *Requiem*, a . . . melancholy and often heavenly piece, with an almost Romantic intensity."[70] And after a performance by Herbert Henck in Cologne, West Germany, critic Eva-Elizabeth Fischer wrote about the work, "An impression of suspended gravity breaks forth, as if the composer wished, with torrents of notes, to overwhelm everything which she had hidden in silence all the years of her life."[71]

Richter's Aesthetics

The 1970s were particularly exciting and successful years of composition for Richter. Her achievements led to an interview by Jane LePage for the book *Women Composers, Conductors, and Musicians of the Twentieth Century: Selected Biographies*. In the interview, Richter gave an extended description of her musical aesthetics:

> There was never a time when I did not think of myself as a musician—first as a pianist, then as a composer and music was always a means of expression for me. I am not a verbal person.
>
> In recent years I have come to realize that this must be the reason I never followed any prescribed theory or system or style of composition. Melodic contour, rather than any formula for tonality or serialization, is the fundamental element in my music. The continuous line from the beginning to the end of each piece is what governs the form.
>
> Each new piece is a new experience for me. Most of the thematic relationships occur subconsciously, spontaneously as I play through the piece and allow, coerce new material to develop. This can be a painfully slow process but when I try to develop new sections by consciously manipulating themes and chords and rhythms, I invariably destroy the work. I have to throw out these constructions and go back to my own system—allowing the music to come from its own mysterious source.
>
> Composing is my response to a constant desire to transform my perceptions and emotions into music. Everything that touches me, everything I become aware of as beautiful or mysterious, or painful, or joyful, or unknowable becomes an immediate or eventual source of inspiration.
>
> A painting, a photograph, a landscape, a skyscape, a poem, other music, other people—my feelings about all of these things filter through my consciousness and take shape as musical ideas and impulses, which must then be expressed.
>
> Music is the way I speak to the silence of the universe.[72]

Richter's constant linking of music to emotional impulses, and the prominence of theme-and-variations form throughout her career, is notable within the broader discussion of feminist aesthetics. Music scholar Renée Cox Lorraine has considered writings by musicologists (Marcia Citron, Eva Rieger, and Susan McClary) and by composers (Miriam Gideon, I'lana Cotton, Annea Lockwood, Ruth Anderson, Pauline Oliveros, and Ellen Taaffe Zwilich) and suggests that there may be a subtle resistance by women composers toward the conventions of sonata form and that some women composers might tend to gravitate to a different type of structure in which extensive development of a limited amount of material is emphasized.[73] At this time, however, it is not possible to generalize convincingly about women composers' expressions and experiences; Richter's music is a personal expression that includes her experiences as a woman but is not limited to them.

5 Expansion
1980s

You can find her work if you seek it out. They might not have it at every record store and it might not be in the top ten, but it takes you places that those top ten hits won't, and they're places worth visiting.

David Garland, remarks on *Evening Music*, WNYC, March 31, 1999

THE COMPOSITIONAL ATMOSPHERE of the 1980s was extraordinarily varied. Some composers continued to compose serial, electronic, and chance music. Others wrote sound-mass music and sound poetry, used environmental sounds, and became performance artists. Richter continued to go her own way. Eager to continue her 1970s success, she wrote primarily symphonic and chamber music but also returned to writing vocal and choral music, all in a richly chromatic language.

English and Irish Influences

In 1980 Richter completed her *Spectral Chimes/Enshrouded Hills* for three orchestral quintets and orchestra. She had begun work on it in 1978 after she received her first National Endowment for the Arts Fellowship to write a piece for Ainslee Cox and the Oklahoma Symphony. The initial working title was "Music for Three Quintets and Orchestra."[1] (In a January 8, 1980, letter to Richter, Skrowaczewski playfully suggested the title *M435aO*.) This was soon expanded to *Music for Three Orchestral Quintets and Orchestra*, to indicate that an orchestra would not have to hire outside quintets but that the quintets, standard woodwind, brass, and string, were drawn from within the orchestra itself.

This twenty-five-minute work is uniquely scored for wind quintet (flute, oboe, clarinet, horn, bassoon), string quintet (2 violins, viola, cello, bass), brass quintet (2 trumpets, horn, trombone, tuba), and orchestra.

In her performance note for the piece, Richter explains:

> The quintets are drawn from the orchestra and should, ideally, be seated at the front of the stage as solo groups. They are employed both as quintet groups and as a pool of 15 soloists functioning in a variety of groupings with and without the orchestra, and at times in unison with the orchestra in concerto grosso style. In short, the quintets do not serve exclusively as separate entities in dialogue with each other or the orchestra. Rather, their function is to "personalize" the thematic material to add a special acoustic and expressive dimension which would not otherwise be present.[2]

Some time after completing the work, she changed the title yet again and added the following to the performance note:

> While writing *Spectral Chimes* I was reading Thomas Hardy's *Tess of the D'Urbervilles*. My consciousness was gradually permeated with the image of Tess constantly toiling up and down those misted English hills, seeking something which proved to be always beyond reach. These feelings are reflected in the music . . . Hardy's references, in his poetry, to phantoms and to tolling bells, became my spectral chimes and his distant vistas my enshrouded hills.

In 1995 Richter traveled to Prague, where the work was recorded, along with her *Quantum Quirks of a Quick Quaint Quark*, by the Czech Radio Symphony Orchestra conducted by Gerard Schwarz. In the liner notes to this recording, composer Mark Lehman suggests that the specific images are not as important as the colorful scoring and more abstract relationships within the work:

> This description may suggest a misty, impressionistic tone-poem, but Richter's composition is much more ambitious, uncompromising, and original than that. . . . The resulting work is a remarkable synthesis of complex scoring, rigorous structural integrity, and deeply-felt emotion that—like Thomas Hardy's doomed protagonists and desolate landscapes—encompasses impassioned defiance, granitic strength, evocative mystery, forlorn majesty, and, ultimately, stoic resignation.[3]

Lehman then provides an extended analysis of the loosely sonata-form movement. His description of the primary theme and its transformations reveals the grand scale of the piece:

> *Spectral Chimes* opens with sound and fury: a rugged fortissimo statement of its main motive, whose repeated notes, skips, and spring-loaded triplet motion will appear again and again, in various guises, throughout the piece, becoming the source of much of its thrusting, impulsive energy.

This allegro theme is divided among the quintets, beginning in the brass quintet, continuing in the wind and string quintets, and returning to the brass quintet. The contrasting secondary theme, introduced at a new andante tempo by a solo trumpet, is accompanied Richter-style with steady ostinatos in the winds and strings.

Interestingly, Lehman refers to minimalism at one point, writing:

> Some of this development is highly contrapuntal, while other parts are less melodic than chordal, as orchestral figurations project an array of slowly-changing verticalities over a steady rhythmic pulse in a sort of quasi-minimalist style (though Richter is far more craggy, dissonant, unpredictable, and passionate than the hedonistic aesthetic of minimalism allows for).[4]

This pseudominimalist, hypnotic effect that Lehman observes occurs in many of Richter's works, such as the *Landscapes of the Mind* series, though Richter herself never identified her music with minimalism, as she thought of the term in the more narrow sense of a Steve Reich–Terry Riley classic minimalist style.

The CD received numerous favorable reviews.[5] In one review David Denton wrote:

> Her orchestral scores show a composer who has a total command of orchestral sonorities, used with considerable panache, and a potent melodic conception.[6]

And of *Spectral Chimes/Enshrouded Hills* specifically, Denton wrote:

> This juxtaposition of chamber-music transparency and the dense quality of the full orchestra captures the frequent moments of desolation in Hardy's novel. The work progresses to a massive and overwhelming climax, just off the center of the work. This makes the work's cold coda all the more harrowing, and it closes in frightening despair and darkness.

In 1999 the CD was featured on a WNYC radio broadcast. Before introducing *Spectral Chimes*, broadcaster David Garland remarked about Richter's music in general:

> Her music has unusual proportions and unusual emphases, and that's just matters of shape. There's also the tonality, which hovers around between tonality and atonality . . . drama and calmness . . . and, it's just an interesting experience, her music. It's a musical journey that you take with her.[7]

EXEQUY

Richter often composed works in response to personal relationships. The two-minute piano piece, *Exequy* (1980), is one of those.[8]

> *Exequy* was written in memory of my father, and embodies a range of emotions from nostalgic tenderness, which characterizes the essential essence of our relationship, to rage, despair, regrets and then the eventual healing that had evolved by the time he died. I was not told of his passing, in September of 1979. When I did not receive my customary

October birthday greetings, I contacted a nephew who gave me the news. The two-minute *Exequy* expresses the resulting violent contrasts of emotions, but ends in calm resignation. Although it begins and ends on an arpeggiated B minor $^6_4$ chord, with an added E♯, which lends an element of repose, the highly chromatic harmonic and melodic elements, rhythmic complexities and fierce dynamic juxtapositions dispel any categorization of it as a small work, in effect. The brief interpolation, at the climax, of thematic material from my *Lament*, written for my mother, ties the two works poignantly together.[9]

The title was taken from a poem by Henry King and added after the piece was written, as were the last two lines of the poem, quoted on the score: "Sleep on, my love, in thy cold bed, / Never to be disquieted."[10] The piece is simple (AA′A″codetta) and in the key of B minor, mostly in $^6_8$ with a right-hand melody accompanied by arpeggiated minor and fully diminished seventh chords in the left hand. Polyrhythms of four against three, and five against four appear at the work's fortissimo climax. (In 1983 Richter arranged the piece for mixed quartet: oboe, clarinet, cello and piano.)

LAMENT FOR ART O'LEARY

In 1983 (on commission from soprano Margaret Willig for a premiere in Tully Hall, New York), Richter set the powerful Irish text, *Lament for Art O'Leary*, for soprano and piano. In her program note Richter writes:

In 1773, O'Leary, an Irish Catholic patriot, was outlawed and murdered in Carriganima, County Cork, by the Protestant Morris, for refusing to sell his valuable horse to him for five pounds. (Catholics were forbidden to own a horse of greater value.) His widow, Eileen, not only wrote the *Lament*, which has been called "as remarkable as anything in Irish literature," but is said to have carried out her threat against the murderers by having them deported and was most likely responsible for having Morris shot by her brother.

The *Lament* is modeled after the traditional *keen*, a primitive, ritualistic custom which developed into a literary form described as "never-ending, intricate genealogical verses" and "a ritual over the dead with characterized characters, story-telling and an implied crowd of cloaked weepers." The complete poem includes many verses attributed to Art's sister in which the widow is taunted, which I have not set. My setting of the remaining 226 lines conforms to the cyclical structure of the narrative. The many varied repetitions of the primary melodic material are separated by short contrasting self-contained fragments and miniatures. While I have not attempted to write "Irish" music, the musical idiom does combine an archaic, modal flavor with 20th-century harmonic freedom and expressive use of dissonance.[11]

Fittingly, *Lament* was premiered on St. Patrick's Day 1996 by Trudy Wodinsky and Richter at Hofstra University. It is dramatically very demanding on the soprano, who must perform it as almost a mini-opera. The vocal part is quite chromatic, yet considerate of the voice, and the accompaniment is somewhat sparse, with rolled, harplike chords at the beginning and the conclusion. In between, when called for, the accompaniment tellingly expresses the turmoil of the text.

A strong climactic point occurs at the words "And your blood in torrents, Art O'Leary, I did not wipe it, I drank it from my palms." The soprano must negotiate leaps of minor and augmented ninths and an ascending glissando of a minor twelfth followed by a free chromatic descent.

Richter's interest in Irish themes would continue in 1995 with her chamber opera *Riders to the Sea* (see chapter 6).

Return to Choral Writing

TO WHOM? SATB (1980)

During the 1980s Richter returned to choral writing after a fifteen-year hiatus, starting with her 1980 work, titled *To Whom?* (for unaccompanied SATB chorus). It was commissioned by the Muse of Eloquence Inc. for the New Calliope Singers (Peter Schubert, conductor) and premiered by them in Alice Tully Hall

12. Marga Richter at rehearsal with conductor Peter Schubert and the New Calliope Singers, with son Michael Skelly at the piano, 1981.

on March 6, 1981. In this work, Richter achieves a masterful blend of music and text, setting a passage from Virginia Woolf's modernist masterpiece *The Waves*.[12] In his *New York Times* review of the performance, critic John Rockwell referred to the work as "evocatively chromatic."[13]

The prose in *The Waves* is particularly well-suited for a musical setting, with its rhythmic structure, repeated phrases, and vivid imagery. Melba Cuddy-Keane describes Woolf's novels as "environmental soundscapes in words" and *The Waves* specifically as "a novel for voices" that Woolf and others had even considered for a radio adaptation.[14] In *The Waves*, Woolf experiments with form and explores the world of inner thoughts. The novel has six characters, three male and three female, who speak in nine sections in soliloquies about their perceptions as they progress from infancy to old age. Each section is preceded by a brief interlude that describes nature and the cyclical passage of time. The sun moves across the sky and the ocean tide changes to suggest the passing of a day, while the changing seasons suggest the passing of a year. Some critics interpret the six characters as different parts of one person.[15]

The passage set by Richter is from a sensual fantasy by Rhoda who wanders down a hedge, gathers flowers, and longs "to present" them. Rhoda's description of her body as a "fertilising" stream expresses female orgasm.[16] Rhoda's character has been analyzed as representing the paradoxical situation of women in opposition to and struggling for authority, and as an exploration of powerlessness, helplessness, and paranoia.[17]

Richter's setting captures the delusional mood of the passage and corresponds sensitively to patterns in the text. After a brief introductory phrase, "Here is a poem about a hedge" centered on an E♭ minor triad, the passage divides into three large sections, each ending with the phrase "Oh! to whom?"

Almost half of the lines begin with the phrase "I will . . ." (as in "I will wander . . . ," "I will clasp . . . ," "I will sit . . ."), or "I . . ." (as in "I faint," or "I am incandescent"). For these phrases, Richter uses a monophonic setting in one voice or two voices, each derived from the opening melody with its winding chromatic pitch pattern broken up by rests, creating a feeling of hesitation. As each phrase continues, the texture increases to between six and eight parts, moving homorhythmically in complex five- and six-pitch dissonant chords toward a final complex chord on "Oh! To whom?"

In general, the registral distribution is mostly in thirds with the parts proceeding slowly outward. The climax of the piece occurs on a complex six-pitch chord, triple forte and diminuendo, in ten parts.

Richter again uses textural contrast effectively by setting an added text phrase

"Kyrie Eleison" polyphonically against the homorhythmic setting of Woolf's text (musically eliding with each "Oh! To whom?" phrase). This *Kyrie* theme is from the beginning of a Mass that Richter began in June 1965 but never finished or went back to. (In 2004, she used the theme again for her *Kyrie* for string quintet or string orchestra.)

The first setting of the "Kyrie" is primarily in D harmonic minor, but becomes increasingly chromatic. The final four-part setting of the "Kyrie" refers back to the E♭ minor harmonies of the opening measures. The insertion of the "Kyrie" text adds a layer of conflict to the Woolf passage that contributes to the sense of inner turmoil.

DO NOT PRESS MY HANDS SSATTB (1981)

Richter's 1981 *Do Not Press My Hands*, text by Chilean poet Gabriela Mistral (1889–1957), was written for the Western Wind vocal ensemble (SSATTB) and premiered by them on June 9, 1981, at the Fourth Festival of Women's Music and the Interart Center in New York. It is the most densely scored of Richter's choral works, and the most chromatic. The sustained chords in the first four measures return transposed at structural points in the text with the words: "Do not kiss my mouth," "Don't touch me, therefore," and "It is in the kiss." Richter's rhythms are sensitive to the nuances of the text, and the variety of textural patterns provides the main interest in the work. As in *To Whom?* the text expresses a woman's point of view and mixes sensuality and spirituality.

THREE SONGS ON POEMS BY EMILY DICKINSON SSAA (1982)

Richter's 1982 *Three Songs on Poems by Emily Dickinson*, (unaccompanied SSAA chorus), is her only work not yet performed. The mystical poems are "God made a little Gentian," "I like to see it lap the Miles," and "'Twas just this time, last year, I died."[18]

In "God made a little Gentian," a gentian (a blue or purplish-blue flower with four or five petals) wants to become a rose. The brief piece is in a simple three-part form with the opening melody returning transposed a half step higher.

In "I like to see it lap the Miles," "it" seems to be a magnificent horse that "step(s) around a pile of mountains" and ends "at its own stable door." Richter captures the horse's gait in her $\frac{6}{8}$ setting and creates a bitonal effect between sopranos and altos. Some whimsical word-painting occurs with the words "horrid hooting," "chase itself down Hill," "neigh," and "stop."

"'Twas just this time, last year, I died," begins mournfully and has the most contrapuntal writing of the three. The contrapuntal sections alternate with sections in which the altos sustain pedal tones under the paired sopranos. The mood changes as the text contemplates "how just this time, some perfect year Themselves should come to me." Richter's setting becomes much less chromatic, settles into G♯ minor, and ends on a hollow G♯ chord. Richter's skill in weaving together highly chromatic passages and more tonal ones creates a seamless quality and high degree of expression in her work.

Arizona-Inspired Work and All-Richter Concert

Richter had composed in response to nature in her *Landscapes* series, *Blackberry Vines and Winter Fruit* and *Spectral Chimes/Enshrouded Hills*. In 1981 she wrote yet another work responding to the beauty in nature, *Sonora* for two clarinets and piano. This time the source of inspiration was the Sonoran desert in Arizona, which she had seen on her trip to Tucson for the premiere of *Landscapes of the Mind I* in 1976. On the origins of *Sonora*, Richter has written:

> When I had the opportunity to compose a piece for the Drucker Trio (Stanley and Naomi Drucker, clarinets and Blanche Abram, piano), for a New York premiere on my proposed All-Richter concert in October, 1981, I immediately recalled my reaction to the Sonoran Desert. This vast, serene landscape is overpowering, yet also seems vulnerable, even fragile, and I wanted to express these feelings in music. The rich but disembodied timbre of the clarinets (in this case, both in A), especially when combined with the sonorousness of the piano, seemed to be the ideal combination of instruments for such a piece. *Sonora* is the result. It is simpler in harmonic texture and formal design than the *Landscapes* series. The structure develops freely, and although there are extreme contrasts in mood, it forms one unbroken arch from beginning to end.[19]

This free-form work illustrates many characteristics of Richter's style: dissonance used for expressive effect, chromatic lines, octave melodies and broken minor and diminished triads often in second inversion, extended trills always to the minor second above, attention to dynamics and articulation, and limited imitation between parts.

In addition to numerous performances by the Drucker Trio, *Sonora* has been played by other trios, in Tucson, Arizona; Evanston, Illinois; Dusseldorf; Paris; and Oslo to name a few locales. In a 1985 *Fanfare* review, *Sonora* was called "a dark, but not somber, piece with the ebb and flow of activity and dynamics . . . a very fine and lovely work," and critic Robert Croan wrote for the *Pittsburgh Post-Gazette*, "*Sonora* . . . exploits the sonority of the clarinet in unexpected and interesting ways."[20]

ALL-RICHTER CONCERT IN MERKIN CONCERT HALL (1981)

With funding from the Martha Baird Rockefeller Foundation, Richter arranged an all-Richter concert to be held at Merkin Concert Hall in New York City on October 18, 1981. The concert consisted of a wide variety of Richter's music played by excellent performers: Sonia Gezairlian Grib, *Soundings*; Curtis Macomber and Richter, *Landscapes of the Mind II*; Peter Basquin, *Sonata for Piano*; the Atlantic Quartet (Linda Quan, Evan Paris, Lois Martin, and Chris Finkel), *String Quartet No. 2*; and the Drucker Trio, *Sonora*.

Theodore Libbey Jr. reviewed the concert for the *New York Times*. Though his review was somewhat harsh toward Richter's music, it did contain some praise:

> In small doses, the music of Marga Richter can be intriguing and enjoyable. Intriguing because it involves the listener in an experience in which he can gauge probabilities with a reasonable degree of accuracy. Enjoyable because it is highly melodic and takes advantage of sustained and accumulated sounds that are often, if not always, kind on the ear. But taken in a large dose, as it was Sunday night at the Merkin Concert Hall, the same qualities that lend Miss Richter's music an appealing predictability—the recurrence of certain rhythmic and melodic trademarks—can take on the appearance of wallpaper, becoming almost pathologically routine.[21]

Despite this review, the high-caliber concert helped to strengthen Richter's presence in the media's and public's eyes.

Visit to Germany and Düsselfdorf Works

In March 1981 Richter received a letter from Francisco Tanzer who had heard her *Requiem* for piano played by Doris Hays (now Sorrel Hays) on a local radio broadcast in Düsseldorf, Germany. He was, in his words, "overwhelmed by the piece," and invited her to compose a work honoring the eminent Russian composer Sofia Gubaidulina for a concert in Düsseldorf that October and to attend the concert at his expense. Richter replied that she was too busy writing a new piece (*Sonora*) for her own concert in October. Tanzer then decided that the Düsseldorfer Ensemble, which he comanaged, would program her *Sonora* and also present her in a special event at the Robert-Schumann-Institut, playing and discussing her *Requiem* and U.S. music in general.[22] So, at age fifty-five, she went overseas for the first time. She used this opportunity also to visit a cousin, Karen Eisfeld, in Hannover, whom she had never met. While there, she visited her father's childhood home in Einbeck (where she also met her father's brother,

Richard), the opera house in Hannover where her mother performed, and the church in which her parents were married.

The performances went well in Düsselfdorf, and Richter was commissioned by the ensemble to compose a new work for them. She wrote her twenty-minute *Düsselfdorf Concerto* for solo flute, solo viola, solo harp, percussion, and string orchestra (1982). The ensemble premiered it in Salzburg, Austria, on May 20, 1982, conducted by Wolfgang Trommer, and performed it later in Düsselfdorf. The work was inspired by her feelings about discovering her roots firsthand and the sorrow she felt as she confronted the fact that she could not share these feelings with her now-deceased parents. She uses themes from Gubaidulina, Beethoven, Schumann, and Brahms, to create her own musical structures. Nostalgia came through most tellingly in her use of a Brahms lied, "O wusst ich doch den Weg zuruck" ("O would that I knew the way back"), that reflects on lost childhood, and the hymn "Open My Eyes that I May See," both of which are included on the only recording she and her mother made.[23]

The *Düsselfdorf Concerto* had its U.S. premiere in 1987 at the New Hampshire Music Festival, directed by Thomas Nee, where Richter was a composer-in-residence.[24] The work received later performances, including one in February 1992 by the San Francisco Women's Philharmonic conducted by JoAnn Falletta. Critic Joshua Kosman disliked Richter's use of quotations, saying "the assemblage made little artistic sense to me."[25] In a review that was largely negative toward the concert as a whole, Paul Hertelendy wrote that "Marga Richter's one-dimensional and repetitive *Düsseldorf Concerto* is a musical diary of reminiscence about her roots in Germany, dominated by endless quotations out of hymnbooks, Schumann and Brahms. Like most diaries, it works best when confined to the drawer of its creator."[26] In contrast to these remarks, reviewer Basil De Pinto called Richter's *Düsselfdorf Concerto* "the most distinguished composition of the evening," noting that "a skillful handling of means resulted in a completely finished work, in no sense a pastiche but the endeavor of a serious artist and composer to contend with."[27] Falletta has described Richter's work in general, saying, "I have always been a great fan of her music—it is strong, individual and communicative."[28]

The work is in three movements to be played without pause. The final movement serves as a resolution and brings back material from the first. Ostinatos help unite the diverse parts as the textures weave between soloistic passages and ensemble passages.

After the success of *Düsseldorf Concerto*, Tanzer commissioned Richter to compose a set of songs to his own poetry. These became her *Sieben Lieder* for soprano and piano (1985). The seven songs are: "Tag für Tag" ("Day after Day"),

"Später einmal . . ." ("Later, sometime . . ."), "Dezember" ("December"), "Gefährtin" ("Companion"), "Spätherbst" ("Late Autumn"), "Allein" ("Alone"), and "Ursprung" ("Origin"). Richter's setting elevates the level of the poetry, which concerns itself with love and death.

In three of the songs, Richter uses material from some of her other instrumental works. "Dezember" takes its thematic material from the main theme of her *Seacliff Variations* for piano quartet, and "Gefährtin" borrows its accompanimental material from the ninth variation of *Seacliff Variations*. "Ursprung," the final song of the cycle, uses both melodic and harmonic material from her *Exequy*.

Richter's settings establish a distinct mood for each poem, the finest of which are the first two. In "Tag für Tag" she uses a sparse accompaniment of sustained chromatic chords to capture the simplicity and static nature of the poem. "Später einmal . . ." provides contrast with its more rhythmic accompaniment in sixteenth-note triplets to its highly chromatic vocal line.

The cycle was premiered by soprano Constance Cooper and Richter at Christ and St. Stephen's Church in New York on February 28, 1985. It received its European premiere at the Robert-Schumann-Institut in Düsseldorf on November 28, 1985, with Lesley Bollinger, soprano, and Paul Heemann, piano.[29]

Descriptive Works

SEACLIFF VARIATIONS FOR PIANO QUARTET

In 1983 Richter was commissioned to write a piano quartet for the Sea Cliff Chamber Players comprised of Hamao Fujiwara, violin; Toby Hoffman, viola; Ko Iwasaki, cello; and Barbara Speer, piano. They premiered the new work, titled *Seacliff Variations* (1984), in Sea Cliff, New York, on March 17, 1984, and recorded it for the Musical Heritage Society in 1989. In a review of the CD, Steven L. Rosenhaus wrote:

> The theme is primarily tonal, in the minor mode, with dissonances used as a means to emphasize rather than as a means to an end. The writing is extraordinarily powerful, building an emotional tension right from the opening notes that rivets you to your seat until the finish. This is not music for the brain, to be analyzed and intellectualized; it is also not musical wallpaper to be put on while you paint the kitchen. You listen to this music with your soul.[30]

Subsequent performances of *Seacliff Variations* were given by chamber ensembles in Massachusetts, New York, Vermont, and Florida.

Seacliff Variations is an eighteen-minute work in one continuous movement consisting of an introduction, a sixteen-measure theme, twelve variations of greatly

13. Marga Richter with son Michael Skelly playing her Variations on a Theme by Latimer, *1983.*

varying lengths and complexity, several short interludes based on the introduction, and a coda, which is the culmination of an ongoing expansion of the closing bars of the original theme. The theme, in B minor, with Richter's trademark chromatic digressions in the second half, is presented by the violin, with minimal accompaniment in the other instruments. It undergoes transformation and rhythmic development as the piece continues. The eleventh variation, for strings alone, is especially beautiful with its slow lyrical lines. Variation twelve is extended considerably and presents the theme with rhythmic vigor in harmonic blocks.

Richter has provided the following program note:

> Most of my recent music has been written as my response to a particular painting, landscape, photograph or emotional experience. The *Seacliff Variations*, however, sprang from purely musical impulses. After I wrote the fairly simple 16-bar theme, and had accepted its

slightly Griegian flavor, I added a short introduction which provided additional contrasting material. Then I let the piece write itself.[31]

VISIT TO CHINA AND TIBET

In 1986 Richter and her husband Alan visited China and Tibet. Skelly was interested in seeing the Tibetan Buddhist monasteries, whereas Richter was inspired by the beautiful landscape and the tension she felt was in the society from the Chinese presence. As a result of the trip, she wrote *Qhanri (snow mountain): Tibetan Variations* for cello and piano, completed in early 1988.[32]

Richter composed her own rather melancholy F minor theme and also incorporated material she derived from a chant she heard outside the Jokhang Temple.

Cellist David Wells and Richter premiered it on July 9, 1991, at the Yellow Barn Festival in Putney, Vermont. They recorded the work in 1992 and it was released in 1994 on a Leonarda CD, which also included her *Requiem* and *Landscapes of the Mind II*. In the CD liner notes Richter describes the work as "a paean to the fortitude and resilience of the oppressed Tibetan people" and continues:

> Outside the Jokhang Temple I had recorded a chanting monk. When I subsequently heard a similar refrain sung by young novices at the nearby Drepung Monastery, I decided to use it as thematic material, although not as the opening theme, for the variations. My chromatic alterations of the original diatonic, but melismatically embellished, chant are an expression of what I perceived to be a deep sadness underlying the cheerful demeanor of the Tibetan people. A fragmented version of this altered motif first appears as a poignant cello incursion at the climax of Variation 1. Various forms of it are heard throughout the piece but not until the second half of Variation 20 is it harmonized with a major triad, giving it, at last, a closer kinship with the original chant and an optimistic, triumphant coloration.
>
> This chant is the only Tibetan *musical* reference in this piece. However, the opening Theme was written during an early morning drive through the Lhasa Valley as the heavy pre-dawn fog slowly lifted, showing first the rich dark brown color of the lower mountains, then gradually clearing to reveal the snowy peaks in all their primordial grandeur, set off against the glowing azure sky.[33]

In a review of the CD, music critic Michael Redmond called *Qhanri* "the jewel of this particular crown," "a startling ritual drama," and "a tour de force for cello and piano employing 'chromatic alterations' of a Johkang Temple chant," and adds that "with this recording, as with Leonarda's other CDs of Marga Richter's music, the label is doing something to remedy the concert scene's neglect of a powerful, original voice."[34] Reviewer Jocelyn Mackey wrote: "The work is highly romantic, and vacillates between action and contemplation . . . [listeners] can revel in its wonderful expression of various moods."[35]

Throughout the 1990s, cellist David Wells continued to champion *Qhanri*, giving lectures on it even after retiring from performance due to Parkinson's disease. He said, "*Qhanri* has been very meaningful to me. It has become a major composition in my life, like a newly found Beethoven sonata. The piece feels like a long novel, in which the two main characters (the two main themes) discuss in twenty variations ideas of deep spiritual and dramatic impact. I find it to be a grand and wonderful work."[36]

OUT OF SHADOWS AND SOLITUDE FOR FULL ORCHESTRA (1985)

Although Richter had received a second National Endowment for the Arts grant in 1979 to write a work for Christopher Keene and the Syracuse Symphony, she did not begin to write the work, titled *Out of Shadows and Solitude*, until August 1981.[37] It was soon put aside, though, when commissions for the *Düsseldorf Concerto*, *Lament for Art O'Leary*, and the *Seacliff Variations* took precedence because of their scheduled premiere dates. She resumed work on *Out of Shadows and Solitude* in 1983 and completed the eighteen-minute one-movement work in 1985. (By then, Christopher Keene had left the Syracuse Symphony.) It was not until September 1988 that a performance opportunity arose. John Corrigliano, then composer-in-residence with the Chicago Symphony Orchestra recommended it for a performance by the Civic Orchestra of Chicago with Kenneth Jean conducting. This was scheduled for December 9, 1988. In Richter's words:

> This was a tremendously exciting moment for me, but it came at a time when our family was totally focused on Alan's struggle with an inoperable brain tumor, diagnosed in June of that year. He reacted to the performance news with great joy, as he always did in regard to my career. The parts for the score needed to be prepared. A copyist was hastily engaged and the score dropped off in New York on our way to Pennsylvania to see how the construction of Maureen's new house was coming along. As I dropped off to sleep that evening, Maureen heard him say to me: "I think you are going to have a great year." Three weeks later his condition worsened, and he was admitted to Sloan-Kettering Memorial Hospital. As I kept vigil in his room and in various waiting rooms, I had no choice but to spread out the orchestral parts to proof-read them. Our son, Michael, told me to not be embarrassed that people would look askance at me, that it was what Alan would want me to do. He died on October 2.[38]

Richter attended the Chicago premiere of *Out of Shadows and Solitude*, and dedicated the piece and performance to Alan with the following program note:

> Like much of my recent music, *Out of Shadows and Solitude* was inspired by a visual image. In this instance it was the flight of the condor over the Andes Mountains of Peru.

The vastness of this landscape, the majesty and grace of this giant bird soaring through uninhabited space, the absolute stillness, left an indelible impression on my mind, and offered a momentary glimpse of the unfathomable mystery of the universe. I held to this image and to the feelings engendered by it throughout the span of the several years it took me to complete the piece (1981–1985).

I would like to dedicate tonight's premiere performance to the memory of my husband, Alan Skelly. Two lines from David Henry Thoreau's *Walden* seem appropriate as a tribute to the man who was my best friend and staunchest supporter for 36 years.

> ". . . and long the afterglow gives light.
> . . . beyond which memory need not go."[39]

The work was recorded in 1996 by Gerard Schwarz and the Seattle Symphony. Peter Bates offers a vivid interpretation of the work in the CD liner notes to this recording (on which Richter is the only female composer):

> Certainly the powerful opening chords of this piece, in expansive semibreves, suggest a majestic soaring bird. The first several minutes create a sense of movement through contrasting dynamics and instrumentation. As thunderous figures alternate with quieter ones, the listener may experience a sense of the vast sky. A palpable tension soon develops between a *pianissimo* ostinato in the violins in concert with an ominous melody first stated by a solo trumpet, then trombone, horns, and finally woodwinds. Delicate countermelodies dilute the tension at first, which then give way to an outburst of portentous *tutti* chords and a battery of percussion. Part of this piece's excruciating tension arises from not knowing what's going to happen next . . . suddenly, *poco a poco*, the tempo picks up and the strings present a galloping motive. Backed by furious woodwinds and percussion, the rhythm becomes more insistent, almost Stravinskian in its inexorable propulsion. Not only does *Out of Shadows and Solitude* contain intriguing contrasts between themes, but within these themes there are cross-rhythms and countermelodies to seize the attention of even the most jaded listener. Perhaps most compelling is the conclusion that, like the wind currents behind the condor, preserves its complexity even while its strength slowly ebbs away.[40]

This symphonic poem format clearly gave Richter an extended opportunity to demonstrate her orchestration skills.

Alan's death plunged Richter into a prolonged state of grief during which time she found it too painful to compose. However, she was able to work on career-related opportunities. She secured a performance of her *Düsseldorf Concerto* by Kenneth Kline and the New York Virtuosi at C. W. Post College (Long Island University), in memory of Alan, on March 12, 1989. She also continued to organize a project (begun well before Alan's death) with the London Philharmonic Orchestra to record her *Blackberry Vines and Winter Fruit* and works by three other U.S. composers (Irwin Bazelon, Donald Erb, and Erik Lundborg), for release by Leonarda.

In the spring of 1989 Richter and the recording producer Marnie Hall went to London to supervise the recording and then drove west through England and Wales, stopping, in particular, to see Stonehenge and the homes of Dylan Thomas and Thomas Hardy, particular favorites of Richter's, and then on to the Aran Islands, off the west coast of Ireland, her ultimate destination. She was again thinking of writing an opera based on John M. Synge's *Riders to the Sea*, which takes place there, and wanted the experience of actually being there. While touring Ireland, aside from the magnificent scenery, they particularly enjoyed the conviviality of the Irish pubs (where Richter developed a passion for Guinness Stout), and writing limericks using the names of the towns they passed through: Dublin, Cork, Killarney, Kerry, Dingle, Tralee, Listowel, Bunratty, Galway, and Drogheda. In 2000 Richter would polish the usable limericks, add four more and set them all for voice and piano (see chapter 7).

Also during this time, Richter adopted a mixed-breed dog and named him Honeybear. She recalls:

> Eleven months after Alan's death, I was still in a fragile emotional state. In September 1989, on a visit to my daughter Maureen in Pennsylvania, this aspect of my life unexpectedly changed. After imbibing a perhaps overly generous scotch-on-the-rocks we, along with my two-and-a-half-year-old grandson Matthew, went to see her neighbors, where they had two accidentally mixed-breed puppies to give away. The consensus was that I should take one. I demurred but one of them was foisted upon me, and lay in my arms for half an hour. When I told Matthew I was considering taking the puppy, he solemnly announced, "I think that would be a very good idea." So Honeybear became part of my life and helped heal my heart. He lived a long and healthy life until the fall of 2002, when he experienced seizures and blindness due to a brain tumor. I brought him to the auditions and rehearsals for the production of *Riders to the Sea* [see chapter 7]. On two occasions after rehearsals I needed, after midnight, to rush him to emergency care facilities. Two weeks before the performance he needed to be put to rest. The cast members showered me with condolences and flowers. I have never had another pet, because it would not be Honeybear.[41]

14. Marga Richter with Honeybear, ca. 1997.

6 Culmination
1990s

> She has a distinctive voice. She thinks musically. There's something wild and strange in her music that I find compelling.
>
> Michael Redmond, interview by Sharon Mirchandani, 2009

DURING THE 1990S, the compositional world was still fragmented with composers working in serial and electronic music, performance art, and numerous other styles. Richter continued to prefer working in traditional mediums and created music for chorus, orchestra, opera, and voice. Her compositions were fewer in number during this decade, but large in scale for the most part. Richter also dealt more explicitly with profound themes in her music during this time.

Recovery

In February 1990, Richter was finally ready to write music again, inspired by the desire to compose a choral work in Alan's honor, after she found two poems marked as his favorites in his copy of a Walt Whitman anthology: "As I Watched the Ploughman Ploughing" and "The Last Invocation." These became the first and sixth movements of the seven-poem cycle, *Into My Heart*. It is for mixed chorus (SATB) and chamber ensemble (oboe, violin, 2 trumpets, horn, trombone, baritone, tuba, percussion) or piano four-hands.

The second movement uses Robert Frost's "Into My Own," another of Alan's favorites. A poem about Alan, titled "light fragment," by his brother's wife Cathleen Schurr, became movement 3. Movements 4 and 5 use "For Something Which Had

Gone Before" written by Maureen (Skelly) and given to her father one Father's Day and "Beethoven's Music" by R. Glenn Martin, a Harvard friend of Alan's. "Into My Heart" by A. E. Housman closed the cycle and provided its title. This poem had been set to music by Alan, unbeknownst to Richter until she discovered it among his papers as she was about to begin writing this work. She immediately decided to use the music as written. In the aggregate, the poems contain images of mountains and ruminations on death and are rather mystical in nature.

The cycle is more romantic and tonal than most of Richter's earlier works, with thematic links among movements, and frequent pedal tones and ostinati in the accompaniment. The tonal scheme emphasizes D minor and its dominant key, A minor. The movements in those keys (movements 1, 2, 4, and 7) are positioned at the beginning, middle, and end of the cycle and their tonality is quite clear. Movements 3 and 6 end in the sharp keys of B major and C♯ minor, respectively, though the degree of tonality is much weaker and they are freely chromatic throughout. Movement 5, an expression of the profundity and strength found in Beethoven's music, mixes G minor and B♭ major, and ends in B♭ minor.

"As I Watch'd the Ploughman Ploughing" (mvt. 1) is a simple setting in A natural minor that captures the feeling of treading in the poem (reminiscent of Brahms's first song in his *Vier Ernste Gesänge*). In "Into My Own," (mvt. 2), a wide-ranging motive is imitated and slowly transformed over a rhythmic ostinato and, at the end, a D pedal tone in the accompaniment. A much more dramatic, extended movement, "light fragment" (mvt. 3) has instrumental interludes that quote from Richter's *Concerto for Piano and Violas, Cellos and Basses* and the opening theme of the second movement of Beethoven's Piano Sonata, Op. 111 (two of Alan's favorite pieces).

"For Something Which Had Gone Before" (mvt. 4), in A minor, is a delicate centerpiece for the cycle. Set in the treble range for sopranos and altos only, it is wistful and touching. The voices sing phrases primarily in harmonic thirds that are separated by brief instrumental (or piano) interludes.

The accents, forte dynamics, and rich chords of "Beethoven's Music" (mvt. 5) capture the strength that Alan Skelly admired in Beethoven's music. The first four notes of "Du Bist der Lenz" from Wagner's *Die Walküre* (Skelly's favorite Wagner opera) are used thematically. The reference to mountains both here and in "For Something Which Had Gone Before" reflects Skelly's love of the mountain view from their summer home in Vermont (where his ashes are buried).

"The Last Invocation" (mvt. 6) begins *sotto voce*, tellingly painting the words "tenderly," "wafted," "noiselessly," "softness," and "whisper." Richter sets the text in close harmonies sung mostly a cappella.

In the final movement "Into My Heart," Richter combined Skelly's melody with a rhythm borrowed from the opening of her *Concerto for Piano and Violas, Cellos and Basses*. The chorus sings entirely in unison with a simple accompaniment suggesting D minor. The unison writing is somewhat suggestive of chant and concludes the work peacefully.

This moving tribute to her husband, in the piano four-hands version, was premiered in April 1991 at a three-day "Women in Music" festival hosted by Georgia State University in Atlanta, with Lynn Schenbeck conducting. The New Amsterdam Singers, conducted by Clara Longstreth, gave the New York premiere, with chamber ensemble, in the Miller Theatre at Columbia University on May 24, 1995. Additional performances were given by the music departments of Hofstra and Tufts Universities and Nassau Community College.

Even though Richter cared deeply about and continued to grieve for her husband, she is not one to stay down for long. She continued on energetically with her life.

Quirkiness

Early in 1991 Richter made contact with Marin Alsop, then the newly appointed conductor of the Long Island Philharmonic. Alsop evinced interest in receiving Richter scores for perusal. Richter sent *Blackberry Vines and Winter Fruit* and *Lament* for strings. In April, Alsop responded that a shorter, curtain-raiser score would interest her, so Richter tossed off her *Quantum Quirks of a Quick Quaint Quark* (1991) in record time, for her: nine days composing the sketch and two weeks for orchestration.[1] It was premiered at a pair of concerts by Alsop and the Long Island Philharmonic on April 25 and 26, 1992. In the program note, Richter described the work: "I see the Quark looking like a composite of Peter Pan and E.T., gleefully touring the starry universe."[2] She used some material from her early dance scores *All Desire Is Sad* and *The Wanderers* and snippets from Soler's *Fandango*. The five-minute work is lighthearted, with a waltz in $\frac{5}{4}$, frequent meter changes, and unusual instrumental pairings.

In 1995 Richter traveled to Prague to oversee a recording of the work, along with *Spectral Chimes/Enshrouded Hills*, by the Czech Radio Symphony Orchestra conducted by Gerard Schwarz. Mark L. Lehman's liner notes for the CD give an illuminating overview of the piece:

> It is—as its title suggests—short, fast, bumptious, and indeed quick, quaint and quirky. If there is irony in this piece—as there certainly is where, for instance, Richter affectionately mocks boogie-woogie, writes a waltz in five-four time, or deconstructs Antonio Soler's *Fandango*—it's

all offered in the spirit of harmless fun and merry good cheer. . . . There is no need to study up on electrodynamic theory to enjoy Richter's Felliniesque carnival tunes, rhythmic vivacity, and playfully clever scoring—apparent right from the opening phrase, a catchy little tunelet played in parallel by the oddest of odd couples—a piccolo and a contra-bassoon![3]

Richter later arranged the piece for solo organ (1992) and for solo piano (1993).

David Denton reviewed the CD: "The contrabassoon quickly sets the scene for this humorous music, and though it has an instant attraction for the listener, it also has an innocence that conceals its awkwardness to perform."[4]

Culmination

Two large-scale works from the 1990s mark the apex of Richter's output to date. They are her triple concerto, *Variations and Interludes on Themes from Monteverdi and Bach* for violin, cello, piano, and orchestra (1992); and her chamber opera, *Riders to the Sea* (1996).

VARIATIONS AND INTERLUDES ON THEMES FROM MONTEVERDI AND BACH FOR VIOLIN, CELLO, PIANO, AND ORCHESTRA (1992)

This forty-six-minute triple concerto is a free-form fantasy in one movement. It was commissioned by conductor Sheldon Morgenstern and the Eastern Music Festival. Upon receiving the score, then titled . . . *Beside the Still Waters: Variations and Interludes*, Morgenstern wrote to Richter:

> What you have written is absolutely wonderful. I sit at my desk and have a fabulous time attempting to learn/study what you have put on paper in such an ingenious and extraordinary manner . . . I am so intrigued by your remarkable creativity that it is difficult to work on other scores. . . . The solo parts do clearly require 1st class players, although the orchestra (or even a lesser professional orchestra) will have no problem. With the possible exception of the solo violin part, the real problems are for the conductor; i.e., adhering properly to your sense of architecture which is a wonderment. I love you in advance . . . I already feel a great musical pleasure.[5]

Richter attended the premier in Greensboro, North Carolina, on July 3, 1993. The soloists were Robert Weirich, piano; Lisa Johnson, violin; and Neal Cary, cello. The work received a standing ovation. Reviewer Abe D. Jones Jr. wrote:

> Running at some 40 minutes, clearly conceived and clearly developed, the piece has extended—perhaps overextended—cadenzas for the individual members of the trio, but beautifully realized segments for the three instruments together. The piano seems to have pride of place, or perhaps merely the most dramatic solo moments, although the cello is a close

> second. . . . . Effective use was made of quotations from Claudio Monteverdi and J. S. Bach, but only as springboards for Richter's own thoughts. Powerful in its moments of doubt, the work was even stronger in its affirmations of faith regained.[6]

While searching for a descriptive title for the piece, Richter had come across a photograph of the Tiffany stained-glass window *Rainbow* that depicts a vibrant rainbow arching over a mountain brook and pond, surrounded by brilliant blue and purple irises. She recalls experiencing "a strong feeling of inexplicable mystery and peace." In the foreground is an inscription from Psalm 23: "He leadeth me beside the still waters. He maketh me to lie down in green pastures." Implicit, for her, was the next line: "He restoreth my soul." She immediately felt that both her music and the window spoke to the feelings of faith lost and regained. She wrote in a draft of her program note, "[The title] was chosen in response to the bittersweet serenity of the Trio-Cadenza which had become, for me, the defining moment in the concerto, a quiet resolution of all earthly (and musical) conflict."[7] Following the premiere, Richter decided to omit the reference to the psalm, out of concern that it might be too specific, and changed the title.

In a program note for the work, Richter describes the origins of *Variations and Interludes*:

> When I began to write this concerto in February 1992, I was sure of only two things: I would use the *Prologue* from Monteverdi's *Orfeo* as the theme for the variations because for years I had loved it, and each solo instrument would have its own cadenza. I then came across one of my cassettes labeled "good improvisation." Having forgotten what I had played, I was surprised to find it was a wildly distorted fantasy on J. S. Bach's C-major *Prelude* from Book 1 of *The Well-Tempered Clavier*. The turbulent nature of this improvisation, with its strange melodic contours struck me as an interesting contrast to the serenity of Monteverdi. The development of this material became the interludes. Three other important thematic elements in the piece are an original theme accidentally akin to the *Dies Irae* and therefore given that designation in this piece, the Chorale with which *Orfeo* ends, and the portentous four-to-five-chord harmonic progressions used as bridges between some sections.[8]

Richter's note continues with a detailed description of the complicated overall structure that includes a brief introduction, the Monteverdi Prologue theme, and twelve variations of the Monteverdi Prologue theme of varying lengths. All of this is interspersed with the "Dies Irae" theme, interludes, the Monteverdi Chorale theme and its eight variations, and four cadenzas.

The Monteverdi Prologue theme is presented simply by the violin and cello soloists accompanied by harp, suggesting a Baroque sound. The four cadenzas, which comprise nearly a fourth of the work, are one for the trio first, followed by separate cadenzas for cello, violin, and then piano.

In the moving trio cadenza, an astonishing moment of repose that seems to be where the previous twenty-five minutes have been striving to reach, the piano plays a variation of the Bach prelude, starting in D-flat minor and moving to D-flat major after four bars. This serves as an accompaniment to variations of the "Dies Irae" theme in the violin and the chorale theme embedded in the harmonic texture in the cello.

The solo cadenzas following the trio cadenza are each virtuosic showpieces. The cello cadenza is modeled after the Bach cello suites, the violin cadenza is in two sections, the first austere and the second more playful with arpeggios and double stops, and the rhapsodic piano cadenza ends with passionate bitonal arpeggios leading into the orchestra's tutti. Numerous thematic relationships connect the cadenzas to each other and to the work as a whole.

The last section of the work, which begins with Variations 11 and 12 and continues with Chorales 7–9, includes a dramatic, full-blown orchestral statement of the opening prologue theme. A coda for the soloists follows, beginning vigorously, and then winding down in a swirl of arpeggios and trills. The concerto concludes peacefully with a gentle ascending harp arpeggio.

In 1997 Richter went to Katowice, Poland, to supervise the recording of the concerto, with Joel Suben, conductor; Robert Weirich, piano; Renata Knific, violin; Pamela Frame, cello; and the Polish Radio National Symphony Orchestra. Because of time constraints, Richter was regrettably able to spend only a few hours in Warsaw on her way to Katowice. During the four days she was in Katowice, she did find time to go by herself to Auschwitz, "a harrowing, revelatory experience." When the recording was finished, her cousin Karen Eisfeld (whom she had met in Hannover in 1982) came with her husband to Katowice, and they took her to the beautiful "must-see" city of Krakow, which, she thought, more than lived up to its reputation. From there they drove to their home in Hannover by way of Dresden.

Richter's triple concerto appeals in different ways to listeners. Critic Robert Tipps wrote about the instrumentation and the cadenzas in an enthusiastic letter to Marga:

> You have written the finest triple concerto I've ever heard!! And I've heard oodles of 'em. . . . Such a marvelous insight [about what can be done] with that almost overly used "tune" [Dies Irae]. I was fascinated by your ability to use it so expressly cast in such sensitive ways. The four cadenzas are unique. Your placement of them is a brilliant solution to often badly

> misplaced attempts in other triple concerti. . . . And the ending? Wow!! I almost cried! Such a beautiful work.[9]

Composer Murray Cohen sent a congratulatory message to Richter in which he draws connections to not only Bach and Monteverdi, but also favorable comparisons to Mahler and Chopin, concluding

> I agree with Avraham [Sternklar] that it is a masterpiece. . . . You achieved a state of grace in writing this piece. It should be widely played throughout America by many orchestral groups since it is of a quality rarely equaled in this day and age.[10]

Pianist Barbara Kupferberg wrote about the work on a more spiritual level:

> The waters run still, but deep, and the rod is heavy and the road is long, but along the way what beauty. The old and the new, they comfort us. How can a piece quite long seem just an introduction to Heaven? Behind each statue of a variation, a glimpse of otherworldliness. . . . Behind each cadence, a New World unearthly in Baroque splendor. . . . Romantic? Modern? A very Renaissance of sound. I loved it.[11]

Richter arranged a solo piano version of the trio cadenza titled *Prelude for Piano (In Memoriam)* (1993). In addition, the trio cadenza was extracted as the separate piece *Elegy* for violin, piano, and cello (1994). These titles were given to evoke a general feeling and are not for anyone in particular.

RIDERS TO THE SEA

With *Riders to the Sea*, a chamber opera for four soloists, Richter again turned to an Irish theme. Richter had first read J. M. Synge's play of the same title in 1957. She recalls being so moved by it that she considered naming her unborn child Maurya, should it be a girl. (Maurya is the name of the lead character in the play.) Her husband dissuaded her, citing its spelling ambiguity. After the birth of their daughter June 26, 1957, they argued for three days until the nurse at the hospital told them: "This child must have a name!" The name Maureen was chosen, and it fits her perfectly.[12] Richter immediately considered composing an opera from the play, but hesitated when her husband said, "Don't even think about it unless you have a commission and a performance date."[13]

During her 1989 trip to London for the recording of her *Blackberry Vines and Winter Fruit*, she returned to the idea and added the Aran Islands to her itinerary. It was not until 1995, however, that she finally researched and contacted various opera companies and funding sources. Eventually, at the suggestion of Minnesota composer Libby Larsen, director Angela Malek of Opera Millennium in Minneapolis was contacted. She was immediately interested in the project, offering a $20,000 commission and scheduling the premiere for November 1996.

In preparation for this work, Richter attended Irish folk concerts and studied over 350 traditional Irish tunes (in what proved to be a vain attempt to find a few to use in her score). In addition, Richter's exposure to her mother-in-law's Irish brogue helped in her feeling for the inflections and rhythms of the text.

The complete piano score was composed during the summer of 1995 in Vermont. Richter followed her usual method of scanning the text and writing the rhythms before writing the music. Melodic lines to fit these rhythms, with minimal harmonies, were written next. Then the complete score was created. The last step was to arrange the score for a small chamber group that would not sound out of place in the humble cottage-setting off the coast of Ireland where the story takes place. She considered various Irish instruments, decided against bagpipes, which she thought were too raucous, and selected flute/piccolo, bodhran (Irish drum), bells (A–B♭–B–C), Irish harp (or concert harp), concert accordion (free-bass and stradella), two violins, viola, and two cellos (quintet or string orchestra).[14] Richter's orchestration has a Celtic sound to it, overlaid with unexpected but poignant chromaticism. She felt that Vaughan Williams's 1936 full-orchestra setting of the same play, with a large orchestra providing sounds of storms at sea, was too overwhelming for the simplicity of the text.[15]

Richter used Synge's play unaltered. She was drawn to this tragic story because it portrays a woman of exceptional emotional strength. As the opera begins, this woman, Maurya, has lost her husband, father-in-law, and four sons at sea. A fifth son, Michael, is missing at sea, and a sixth son, Bartley, is about to take two horses by sea to sell at a fair in Connemara. Disregarding Maurya's pleas that he not go because of stormy weather, he departs and drowns before he can set sail. Michael's death is confirmed when his clothes are found on a body at sea. Maurya stoically gathers her two daughters around her and the opera closes with the lyric "No man at all can be living for ever, and we must be satisfied."

Unfortunately, the funding for the premiere fell through just a few weeks before the work could be produced. Malek recalled:

> I applied for funding for a triptych of chamber operas, including Marga's "Riders." Unfortunately, we were not successful. The funding climate at the time in Minneapolis was one of political correctness. Our first opera, *Goddess Songs*, met all the criteria being feminist, multi-cultural, etc. Unfortunately, the next operas, including Marga's, did not fit this bill. I grew weary of this artistic confinement in the Twin Cities and moved to Europe shortly thereafter! I don't specifically remember a dollar amount for her work. The theme, albeit heavy, was within the context of the other operas which were lighter. I played through the score and found it musically primal, appropriate to the rawness of the text.
>
> . . . I don't recall how I learned of Marga, because I was looking at a great deal of scores

> at the time. Quite possibly I found out about her through the Minnesota Composers Forum, which is now the American Composers Forum. Maybe she remembers. My memory of Marga was that she was a passionate, typically eccentric creative spirit. I liked her work, and money was the only barrier that prevented us from producing her.
>
> Regarding feminism, I don't know if I found Marga particular political, and *Riders* was quite a different theme to feminism. I think I was just looking for a woman composer at the time and was going in new directions other than feminism or any political themes. I just wanted quality and beauty.[16]

The cancellation of the premiere was, of course, a huge disappointment. Richter's reaction was to begin a series of presentations of selected scenes, with piano accompaniment (to be used as a marketing tool) on LICA programs, starting in November 1996 and culminating in March 2002, by which time the entire opera had been performed. Immediately after this last performance, soprano Julie Nord, who had sung the roles of both sisters (in the same concert) at these concerts, was suddenly inspired to announce that she would mount a fully staged production of the work on the Music at St. Mark's concert series (at St. Mark's Episcopal Church in Jackson Heights, Queens, New York), of which she was director. (Marga fondly recalls bringing Honeybear to the rehearsals.)

The opera received two well-attended performances on December 6, 2002. It was conducted by Gregory Buchalter, an assistant conductor with the Metropolitan Opera, and directed by Emily Zahniser. The cast included: contralto Melissa Maravell (*Maurya*), soprano Susan Holsonbake (*Nora*), mezzo Melissa Perry (*Cathleen*) and tenor Aram Tchobanian (*Bartley*). In 2006 the work was recorded by Leonarda Records with Maravell, Holsonbake, and Tchobanian reprising their roles, Anna Tonna singing *Cathleen*, and Daijiro Ukon conducting. The CD was released in 2011.

Transcendentalism and Love

In September 1990, Ken Burns's PBS documentary film series *The Civil War* captured the attention of forty million viewers, including Marga Richter. Shown in the film was a famous letter written by Major Sullivan Ballou to his wife Sarah one week before he was killed at the First Battle of Bull Run, July 21, 1861. The hint of transcendentalism in the letter and its passionate and touching tone appealed to Richter. She set the following excerpt for medium voice and piano, using a phrase from the letter as the title, *Sarah do not mourn me dead* (1995):

> I have, I know, but few and small claims upon Divine Providence, but something whispers to me—perhaps it is the wafted prayer of my little Edgar—that I shall return to my loved

ones unharmed. If I do not, my dear Sarah, never forget how much I love you, and when my last breath escapes me on the battlefield, it will whisper your name.

Forgive my many faults, and the many pains I have caused you. How thoughtless and foolish I have oftentimes been! How gladly would I wash out with my tears every little spot upon your happiness.

But, O Sarah! If the dead can come back to this earth and flit unseen around those they loved, I shall always be near you; in the gladdest days and in the darkest nights . . . always, always, and if there be a soft breeze upon your cheek, it shall be my breath; or the cool air fans your throbbing temple, it shall be my spirit passing by.

Sarah do not mourn me dead; think I am gone and wait for thee, for we shall meet again.[17]

Written without a key signature, Richter's *Sarah do not mourn me dead* is very sensitive to the text in a freely chromatic style that loosely suggests tonal centers of C♯ minor, D minor, E♭ minor, D major, C minor, and A major, with fluid transitions between the sections. The singer's opening melody, a sequence of mournful chromatic descending fragments, is intensified when it returns rhythmically varied in a new meter, with the text "How gladly would I wash out with my tears." The following declamatory section, "But, O Sarah!" is set in a contrasting melodic style based on rising leaps of thirds, sixths, and fourths. The rhythms of the song flow naturally in a simple narrative style that allows the text to come to the fore. The ending is bittersweet, oscillating between C♯ minor and A major.

Julie Nord and Richter premiered *Sarah do not mourn me dead* on June 9, 1995, at the South Huntington Library on Long Island, and tenor William George and pianist Mitchell Kirker gave the New York premiere on April 26, 2003, for a NewMusicNewYork "Songs of New York" concert in CAMI Hall.

Purpose of Music and Compositional Process

In 1996 classical radio announcer and producer Bruce Duffie interviewed Richter about her music. Richter does not often talk about religion, but in this interview a revealing exchange developed midway concerning her thoughts regarding music and God:

BD: What is the purpose of music?

MR: Oh boy. . . . *[Pause]* Well, I'd like to say something really embarrassing. When I listen to music, I like to close my eyes and just listen because if I'm at a concert it's so distracting when you watch what's going on. One night at a concert, my son played a Schubert sonata, and it was so beautifully done. He's a wonderful pianist, and I felt that the piece had to be written to prove the existence of God. That's a little strange to say, but it feels like it has something to do with that.

BD: I think that's a wonderful feeling and a wonderful way of looking at it . . .

MR: . . . To go back to David Wells and the cello piece, we rehearsed it two or three times just getting the notes, and then one day the music came to him and he just looked at me and said "You know, God has spoken to you in this piece and now he's spoken to me." That was just so beautiful. There you have it.

BD: Maybe we should encourage composers to remember that God is part of the creative process.

MR: Mm hmm. Right.

BD: Is there something inwardly or outwardly spiritual about the music that you write?

MR: I would think so. It's a hard thing to put into words because if you could put it into words, you wouldn't have to have the music. Like I said, my music comes from within. I write it from the inside out, so it has to have something to do with the spirit.[18]

As in this interview, Richter often describes her work as beginning with a sudden overwhelming urge to compose or feeling compelled to compose by an internal force. The specific impetus might come from a relationship, an experience or the desire to reflect the sheer beauty of an image, but Richter seems to feel that there is something profound and spiritual behind the universe and that her music ultimately comes from that. However, she is reluctant to put into words a more specific label for that force.

In a 1998 interview with pianist You Ju Lee, Richter described her compositional process:

> [My compositional style] is essentially melodic, although it may seem dissonant and fragmented at first. I strive for patterns of inevitability, and although well-schooled in traditional harmony and counterpoint, I compose by ear, never adding a single note without playing through from the beginning. This is admittedly time-consuming, but is necessary for me in building the inner logic and final acceptability as a whole greater than the sum of its parts.[19]

Richter has often reiterated this kind of description, that, although she does sometimes revise her works, she composes with a feeling of certainty that she will find or discover exactly the right note, or chord.

7 Blooming
2000s–Present

I recall your music as having a poetic sensibility beyond poetry.

Paul Rapoport to Marga Richter, email 2010

SINCE THE YEAR 2000, Richter has composed music of a more intimate nature, employing a simpler harmonic and melodic language but still embodying her distinctive voice. These works include several song cycles, some of a humorous nature, a variety of chamber music, a return to solo piano music, and two unaccompanied woodwind pieces (clarinet and oboe). Almost all of them were commissioned, and all have been performed. One of them, *Threnody* for string trio, was written in memory of her father, and several others were written in response to the emotional turmoil of a romantic interlude that deepened but then cooled (*Air #1*, *Three Improvisations for Piano*, *Regrets* for piano, and *Kyrie for Strings*). Richter considered this relationship one more source of inspiration for composing emotionally charged music.[1]

Also since 2000, Richter has learned to use a computer music-notation program (Sibelius), and in 2011 established her own Web page, margarichter.com. Her enthusiasm for life in all of its dimensions remains in full force.

Humorous Works

Richter is known by her friends as having a subtle sense of humor, enjoying wordplay, puns, and oddities. (She is especially fond of the 2003 book *Eats, Shoots and*

Leaves by Lynne Truss, a hilarious collection of misplaced punctuation.) While much of her music is dark and somber in mood, her fanciful humor shows up in a variety of pieces from this time.

In the spring of 2000, Richter turned to the limericks she had written during her 1989 trip to Ireland, wrote a few new ones in order for the set to match her complete itinerary, and set all of them to music, creating a funny and personal song cycle called *Erin Odyssey*. ("Erin" is another name for "Ireland.") Most of them rhyme with the name of the town in question, and some of them describe actual events. The following selection from the set shows Richter's skill at imaginative rhyming and narrative:

To wit (no pun intended):

"DUBLIN"

Marga Richter, the Long Island composer,
Found out that *here* nobody knows her.
    She took to Guinness,
    Which she drank to excess,
And became famous for shameless exposure.

"DINGLE"

When they came to the village of Dingle,
They flirted with posting this jingle:
    "Since we're without mates
    We'd like to have dates,
But only with men who are single."

So, hoping with natives to mingle,
They set out with nerves all a-tingle.
    They imbibed at a pub,
    And consumed some fine grub,
But alas, in the morn no new ingle!

"BUNRATTY CASTLE"

There was once a soused knight at Bunratty
Obsessed with becoming a daddy.
    Up and down the back stairs
    He showed ladies his . . . wares . . .
But was too drunk to sire a taddy.

"WALES"

Then they travelled to London through Wales,
Any verbal description of which pales.

Those inns extraordinarily ensconceable
In towns exceedingly unpronounceable
Provided a fitting finale to these tales.[2]

The music is very simple, with folklike melodies accompanied by mostly primary chords. Although *Erin Odyssey* is set in mezzo-soprano range, contralto Melissa Maravell and Richter premiered the set on November 19, 2000, at the Huntington Public Library on Long Island. The work was also performed for a Sigma Alpha Iota—Albuquerque (NM) Alumnae Chapter Annual American Music Concert, on February 16, 2002, by Julie Rombach-Kendall, soprano, and Marion Henry, piano.

Richter's *Bye-Bye Bake Shoppe* for narrator and string quartet was written in 2005 as part of a Long Island Composers Alliance project pairing local composers with poets and authors to create pieces for children's concerts. The text by U.S. poet Elisabeth Raine whimsically describes the travails of an aged baker reluctantly closing his shop and frantically instructing the pies, cakes, and ingredients to quickly leave. Its twenty-two verses contain musical allusions and entertaining references to places in New England, the West Coast, Miami, France, and even Beirut. Richter inserts well-known musical quotes ("East Side West Side" and "They Wore No Pants in the Hoochie Coochie Dance") for comical effect, and uses word painting on numerous words such as "bend" and "scream," and pizzicato to give the effect of creeping about. It is a droll, effective work. Here is a sampling of the verses:

Now boogie out the bakery door . . .
It's really time to skeddadle.
We must all find a place to go . . .
I'm headed to Seattle.

So the pies went to Poughkeepsie,
The cakes went to Cape Cod,
The muffins to Miami . . .
The bagels prayed to God.

The salt ran off with the pepper,
The nuts are headed for New York,
The yeast started rising
But got punctured by a fork!

The cream cheese started crying,
The jellies are in a jam,
The apron strings got so tangled up
They knocked down all the pans!

The doughnuts all went downtown
And the frosting flew to France.
Now the bake shoppe is getting empty
And the ants are doing a dance.[3]

Bye-Bye Bake Shoppe was premiered by Christopher Linn and the Transfiguration Quartet in Riverhead, Long Island, on March 5, 2005. In January 2006, the Tufts Symphony Orchestra gave two performances of it in Costa Rica (San José and the Guanacaste region) and one in Medford, Massachusetts, for children's concerts.

In March 2005, Richter met Randy and Eileen Lee at a party given by an old friend, Paulette Leibowitz, who had been a piano student of hers in the late 1940s. Richter recalls, "They were skeptical of my credentials as a composer to be reckoned with. I set them straight, suggested they commission me to write a piece for them, and they did! I immediately decided it was time to write this silly piece I had been toying with for fifteen years, with movements having titles with two meanings, one about the seashore, the other a like-sounding word referring to musical terms or well-known music by other composers, snippets of which are quoted."[4] The resulting work was Richter's *Divers (Diverse) Divertimento* for flute (bass flute), oboe/English horn, and guitar (2005), in sixteen movements:

1. Low Tide (Tied)
2. The Mussel Offering (The Musical Offering)
3. Crab Canon
4. The Goldfish (The Goldberg) Variations
5. Coral (Choral) Reef (Beethoven's Ninth and Handel's Messiah)
6. Scales (Descending)
7. Rock Bottom (Rock of Ages + Rach. 3)
8. Ground (Round)
9. Bass Area (Bass Aria—Non piu andrai)
10. Grave (Nearer My God, to Thee)
11. High Tide (Tied)
12. Reel (Irish—The Dogs among the Bushes)
13. The Rapture of the Deep (Ballet of the Pixilated Penguins)
14. Air
15. Reeds
16. Holy Mackerel (Holy, Holy, Holy)

Again, as in *Bye-Bye Bake Shoppe*, word-painting and musical puns abound. The references are detailed in her program note in the score, along with the following scenario for the work:

> Three deep-sea divers arrive at the beach at low tide. They dig up a basket of mussels, watch a crab scurry forward and then backward, pause to watch a school of goldfish inhabiting the

> coral reef, which sadly is disintegrating, then admire the scales of other colorful fishes they pass as they slowly descend to rock bottom. Bounding about on the ground they admire a few sea bass, and then stumble upon a grave. After a few quiet respectful moments they decide to take advantage of the high tide to ascend and ask to be reeled up. Upon reaching the beach again, they are greeted by a few friendly dogs that crowd around them while they struggle comically to regain their physical balance and mental acuity. Finally able to relax and breathe in the fresh air, they contemplate the day's activities, admire the reeds along the shore and realize they have had a great adventure.[5]

The piece was premiered by the Constellation Trio (Linda Wetherill, flute/bass flute; Terry Keevil, oboe/English horn; and Steve Salerno, guitar) on September 10, 2005, at the Vail-Leavitt Music Hall in Riverhead, New York. Richter's *Regrets* for solo piano (2005) is an earlier form of the tenth movement, Grave, and *Air, No. 1* for solo piano is an earlier form of the fourteenth movement.

Another of Richter's humorous pieces, *Not Your Grandmother's Four-Hand Piece* (2006), was cowritten with a colleague, George Cork Maul. Using the Sibelius music notation program, he wrote a four-bar phrase and emailed it to her. She added a phrase or two and sent it back. As this process proceeded, each of them would occasionally make changes to the other's efforts. Richter described it: "Arguments sometimes ensued, when my chromaticism clashed with his neomodalism, but were eventually settled amicably, albeit with a soupçon of sarcasm in some cases."[6] The two have enjoyed playing the work, which at one point requires the secondo player to gradually slide to the right on the piano bench as his part rises into the treble clef, thus forcing the primo player to get up and scurry around to sit on the left side of the bench. Lively rhythms, abrupt changes in tempo, textures, meters, and moods, and imitation between the players, add to the fun. Richter and Maul premiered the piece on February 26, 2006, at the Southold Free Library on Long Island and played it on several occasions thereafter, and the Felsenthal-Vandersall Duo gave the New York premiere at the Donnell Library Center on May 20, 2007.

Also in 2006, Richter set a group of six poems by Marcia Slatkin, a fellow Long Islander. They met at a performance of Richter's *Three Improvisations for Piano* at a recital by Anne Taffel in Greenport, Long Island. Slatkin commissioned Richter to select and set poems from her book, *A Woman Milking*, inspired by her experience as a backyard farmer for eight years, raising goats, ducks, and hens. Richter chose only those poems about goats and titled the set *Goat Songs*.

Humorous, but also poignant and metaphorical, the poems, each one a moving vignette, deal with birth, eating, empty-nest syndrome, and death. They are: "Cloud," "Gourmet Eating," "Mid-wifery," "Wages," "Comfort," and "The Virtue of Knowing One's Mind." Richter uses drones, clusters, distorted waltz rhythms, and creative rhythms to capture sensitively the quizzical looks, playfulness, grinding jaws, stamping of the feet, and general stubbornness of goats. Melissa Maravell premiered the songs with Richter at the piano at a Long Island Composers Alliance concert at the Southold Free Library on Long Island, February 26, 2007. In the future, Richter may set a selection of Slatkin poems dealing with caring for her mother as she struggled with Alzheimer's disease.

Serious Songs

In 2001, Maravell commissioned Richter to compose the song cycle *Testament* (for contralto, English horn, and piano). This cycle consists of eight songs: "Testament," "Within the Wave," "Ascent," "Presentiment," "Alms," "The Stone," "Presence," and "Even." These songs were settings of poems from Anne Morrow Lindbergh's *The Unicorn and Other Poems* (1956). Anne Lindbergh, the wife of aviator Charles Lindbergh, was both an aviator and the author of thirteen books including novels, diaries, poems, and reflections on her travels. The poems address the pain of loss from a woman's perspective. The italics in the first poem, "*But how can I live without you?*," are a cry from the heart (probably Lindbergh's own) that Richter selected and added to the subsequent poems, except number seven, to unify the cycle. The unrelenting intensity, despair, transcendence, self-abnegation, and visionary insights of the poetry are matched by the music, which is a typical Richterian blend of tonal centers overlaid with stabbing chromaticism. The vocal line is alternately highly dramatic or achingly subdued. The songs "Ascent" and "The Stone" are the anchor pieces of the twenty-minute set, due to their complexity and depth.

Richter's interest in Eastern poetry, which had begun with *Transmutation* and *Two Chinese Songs*, returns with her longest song cycle, at about forty-seven minutes, *Dew-drops on a Lotus Leaf* (2002), for countertenor or tenor and string quartet or piano. The texts, by the Japanese poet and Buddhist priest Ryōkan (translated into English by Jakob Fischer), are about nature and his daily life. The cycle's thirty-nine mostly short songs are grouped according to the seasons, beginning and ending with spring, plus a prologue and an epilogue. The prologue is a complete entity and may be performed by itself (as may any of the sections or individual songs). Melissa Maravell premiered the prologue, with Richter, at a Sounds of Japan concert at the Unitarian Universalist Fellowship of Huntington on April 20, 2002. The complete cycle, with William George and the Long Island

String Quartet, which commissioned it, was premiered on September 10, 2003, in Brooklyn, New York (Borough Hall).

An exquisite work, *Dew-drops on a Lotus Leaf* aptly expresses the simplicity, the wit, and the serene beauty of the texts using simple harmonies in a somewhat modal setting. Richter wrote it with the support of the New York State Council on the Arts Decentralization Regrant Program and the Suffolk County Department of Economic Development.

In 2007 Richter was commissioned by NewMusicNewYork to set two Shakespeare sonnets for a concert titled "21st-century Shakespeare: Chamber Music Inspired by the Bard for the New Millennium." Richter writes in her program note:

> I chose Sonnet CXXVIII because I could easily identify with the sentiments portrayed . . . those of a diffident lover hovering over his inamorata but too shy and inexperienced to act on his deepest desires. I also liked the vivid descriptions of the physical act of playing the harpsichord. And it presented the opportunity to write light-hearted music, because of the antic wit.
>
> Sonnet LXXI seemed to me to be a fitting companion piece to CXXVIII. The conquest consummated, the protagonist heroically and nobly provides his beloved with a way to carry on with dignity should he be the first to die.[7]

The sonnets were premiered by William George on Tuesday, May 1, at St. Peter's Lutheran Church near the Citicorp Center in Manhattan.

"Bloom where you are planted": Chamber and Solo Works

Although Richter has had what many would consider an enviable career, like any composer she would like to see still more high-profile performances and acknowledgment of her work. She occasionally half-jokes, "I'm still waiting for a performance in Carnegie Hall or by the New York Philharmonic." She does believe that her work will earn greater fame eventually.

Richter's son Michael Skelly reflects:

> She clearly thinks of herself as in the tradition of Beethoven and Shostakovich . . .
>
> She doesn't think that women are likely to write music in a different way. . . . She was trying to fit into the tradition of the greats. She thinks she deserves to be considered in that tradition.[8]

Richter has said that while sometimes it is depressing that her music is not more widely known, mostly she has tried to follow the old cliché of "bloom where you are planted." Now in her eighties, she is still intensely active and dedicated to her composing. She receives frequent commissions and has steadily produced and received performances of numerous old and new chamber and solo works. She also coproduces four to five concerts a year for LICA.

Richter returned to writing music for solo piano, beginning in 2003 with a short piece titled *Air*. In her words:

> In A minor, it has a wistful continuous melody over a constant broken-chord accompaniment, which asserts itself with a sprinkling of chromaticism as the piece builds to a sighing climax and then slowly subsides.[9]

She then arranged this piece as a duet for oboe and bassoon (*Air #2*), as part of a proposed wind quintet. In 2004 she made yet another version, this time for flute, oboe, and guitar (*Air #3*), for inclusion as one of the movements in her *Divers (Diverse) Divertimento*.

The *Three Improvisations* for piano (2004) are more romantic sounding than her somewhat thorny *Sonata* for piano. Richter describes her compositional process:

> The impetus for writing the *Improvisations* was simply to add a work of medium difficulty to my catalog of pieces for solo piano. The source of inspiration was a wellspring of wistful longing and nostalgia. My method of composition was to turn on my tape recorder and improvise at the piano, playing whatever came to hand, or mind. I actually woke in the middle of the night to write the first one. When I played the tape in the cold light of day, with the exception of two places where I shook my head in horror at the choice of notes only to find that those notes had been quickly replaced by acceptable ones, thus validating my judgment twice, I was happy to find most of it to be quite usable, with only a little judicious pruning and development. Improvisations Two and Three were created in the same manner, but not nocturnally.[10]

The first improvisation, about four minutes long, is Chopinesque. It freely explores within D harmonic minor, goes through several changes of mood with unstable tonalities, lingers on the D♯ fully diminished seventh harmony, and ends quietly, unresolved with mode mixture on an A major-minor seventh chord with an added C♮. The second one, about six minutes long, is essentially a toccata, with propulsive rhythms, irregular accents, and dramatic changes in dynamics and moods, including a slow ethereal pianissimo stasis, with trills in the right hand that evolve into tremolos over tremolos in the left hand. The movement ends with a bravura flourish. The third one serves as a soft, poignant epitaph. It is slow (a quarter note equals 42), and only twenty-two measures long. A winding chromatic melodic line rises and falls over a constant C♯ minor pedal tone plus a C♯ minor first-inversion chord that changes subtly at points of expressive tension.

The *Three Improvisations* were premiered by Richter in Greenport, Long Island, in June 2004, and she continues to perform them on occasion. Anne Taffel has performed them a number of times on Long Island and in concerts in Laugaborg and Reykjavik, Iceland; in Cuzco, Lima, and Piura, Peru; and in Beijing, China. Christopher Oldfather played them in Hewlett, Long Island, and Dallas, Texas.

Richter's *Kyrie* for string quintet (2004) is for the less common scoring of first and second violin, viola, cello, and double bass. In a chromatically inflected D minor, the work begins softly with a syncopated motive on a low D in the double bass, over which the other strings gradually enter, crescendo, and then subside before the main theme is stated in the cello. The rhythmic motive functions with slight alterations as an ostinato throughout the piece, and the main theme is the same *Kyrie* theme used in *To Whom?* (see chapter 5), now greatly expanded. The work builds to a dramatic fortissimo climax featuring a statement of the theme in octaves: cello in its low register, double bass an octave above it, in its high register—a telling sonority. The piece then gradually dies away, in an extended coda echoing the opening introduction. *Kyrie* may also be played by string orchestra.

Richter's *Fandango Fantasy* (2006) for piano, clarinet, violin, and cello is a more extended chamber work from this time. The work expresses an electrifying rhythmic excitement with its irregular meter, accents, echoing between various instrumental combinations, rhythmic repeated figures, and trills. This work is an homage to Antonio Soler's keyboard masterpiece *Fandango*, from which she borrows melodic, harmonic, and rhythmic figures, some verbatim and others greatly altered. She writes:

> My improvisatory *Fantasy* intertwines these fragments with motifs of my own. For the first two-thirds of the piece the dance-like, sometimes whimsical, quality of the Soler is preserved. Then the piece gradually darkens and gradually becomes slower, more introspective, meditative. It ends pianissimo.
>
> The textures of my *Fantasy* were deliberately chosen to show their provenance, especially in the piano writing, which deliberately eschews virtuosity in favor of subtlety and rhythmic incisiveness.[11]

Fandango Fantasy was written for the Antares Piano-Clarinet Quartet, the 2002 Concert Artists Guild International Competition winners. It was premiered by them (Vesselin Gellev, violin; Rebecca Patterson, cello; Garrick Zoeter, clarinet; Eric Huebner, piano) at a concert on February 11, 2007, at the Park Avenue United Methodist Church in New York. About the performance, Patterson remarked: "The audience loved the work. I recall liking her sensitivity very much

. . . and playing for her—we liked that she had a clear concept of what she was wanting to express."[12] The work has been performed by several other ensembles, including the American Chamber Ensemble (Blanch Abram, piano; Eriko Sato, violin; Chris Finkel, cello; Naomi Drucker, clarinet), which now includes it in its standard repertoire.

In 2007 Richter received a second grant from the New York State Council on the Arts Decentralization Regrant Program, this time to compose her *Serenade for Flute, Percussion and Harp*, for the ensemble Percussia. It is a one-movement work in rondo form featuring a gentle Peruvian-inspired original folklike melody and basically in E minor throughout, with Richter's customary chromaticisms. The music between the four varied returns of the melody is lively and increasingly intense. A solo harp cadenza leads into the last wistful return of the theme, which is half as fast as the original. The piece ends quietly on the dominant. The work was premiered by Percussia (Margaret Lancaster, flute; Ingrid Gordon, percussion; Karen Strauss, harp) at a LICA concert at the South Huntington Public Library on Long Island on November 10, 2007.

For the annual LICA Music for Students concert, Richter often composed small works. One of these was her *Trio* for alto sax, baritone horn, and piano (2006). It is a playful one-movement work in D minor that opens with imitation between the parts. The sax and horn are used more melodically, and the piano rather percussively. Another piece was Richter's *Two Pieces for Two Violins* (2008),

15. Marga Richter rehearsing Fandango Fantasy *with Antares Piano-Clarinet Quartet, 2007.*

which begins with a gentle A minor Pavane in which the two violins are equally balanced, crossing parts frequently. The second piece, *Tag for Two*, which humorously quotes "Tea for Two" (from the musical *No, No, Nanette*) is playful and interactive, like the game of Tag. The two violins have energetic runs together at intervals of fifths, thirds, or tri-tones, and then alternate short phrases that occasionally overlap, as though they are "tagging" each other, before ending in A major.

In the spring of 2008, Richter compiled an attractive set of moderately difficult pieces for piano, *Four Miniatures for Piano*. "Homage J. S. Bach," "March Berserk," "Valse Melancolique," and "Toccatina" may be played individually or as a set. "Homage J. S. Bach" is an ariettalike melody over quasi-Baroque harmonies in block chords. The comical "March Berserk," a revision of Richter's 1945 piece, has spiky harmonies and off-beat rhythms. In the middle, she uses eight bars from the lullaby she wrote for Mary Howell Brinkman's baby, in 1942 (see chapter 1). "Valse Melancolique" is vaguely Impressionistic and Chopinesque. "Toccatina" is hard-driven and virtuosic. She premiered the set on a May 4, 2008, LICA concert at the Southold Free Library on Long Island.

Downsizing

In the fall of 2008, Richter decided to put on the market the large house she had lived in for fifty years (a converted concrete carriage house on the one-time August Heckscher estate on the east side of Huntington Bay), and move to a smaller one. She sold her house in two days and within three weeks found a little white cottage, with a small gnome figure in the front yard, in a quaint, artistic neighborhood on the west side of the harbor, less than four miles from her old house. She referred to her new place as her "elf house" and moved in on April 25, 2009. Always social, she soon made friends in the neighborhood, found walking partners, and began to host small "garden" parties. During the relocation period, Richter continued to compose, supervise performances of her works, and participate as pianist.

An important work from this period is her *Threnody* for string trio. Richter describes its impetus:

> Although I had written a short piano piece (*Exequy*) in 1980 in response to the unexpected death of my father (the notification of which was kept from me until I inquired about him from a family member) in about 2005 I began to think about writing a more substantial work to express our special bond which had frayed a bit in the 1970s, but had healed by the time of his death. I thought of this as an homage and a companion piece to the *Lament* I had written when my mother was dying. A work for piano and small orchestra featuring

oboe and French horn suggested itself, but no actual music was written. Then, in 2008 I was commissioned by the American Chamber Ensemble to write a work for them, preferably for string trio, and *Threnody* is the result.[13]

About twelve minutes in length, *Threnody* begins quietly with a slow, solemn eight-measure introduction in D minor in common time, all in half notes. The melody is divided into two four-measure phrases, the first one in the violin, the second in the cello, as the top voice. Two themes dominate the work: a slow beseeching sighing motive in $\frac{7}{8}$ meter, variants of which are used throughout the piece, in contrasting dynamics, tempi, and dramatic intent; and a second, lyrical theme first introduced in eighth notes by the cello, and then expanded to soaring dotted quarter notes over agitated sixteenth-note accompaniment figures. Mood changes are frequent and unexpected, culminating in a fortissimo return to the opening introduction, expanded to twelve measures and ending softly on an unresolved half-diminished seventh, followed by a return to the sighing theme. An extended coda brings the work to a pianissimo close on an A-minor six-four chord reiterated nine times while the viola plays a thematic E–G♯–G♮–F♯–E. The work was premiered at a LICA concert at the Park Avenue United Methodist Church in New York City on May 3, 2009.

Richter's *Kyrie* for strings was performed in a concert by the Great Neck High School orchestra on May 20, 2009, which the composer was pleased to attend. For a LICA concert on June 5, 2009, Julie Nord performed Richter's *Transmutation* from 1949, and Richter and George Maul performed their *Not Your Grandmother's Four-Hand Piece*. In yet another performance, William George sang two Richter songs for a concert celebrating the fortieth anniversary of the Apollo moon landing on July 11, 2009, Moon Landing Day, at the Tenri Cultural Center in New York City; he sang one of her earliest songs, *Midnight*, and a commissioned newly composed song called "wild moon" to a text by her longtime friend Phyllis Latimer Roberts.

Richter composed her *Summer Reveries on a Mountainside* for solo clarinet in 2010. She describes the impetus for the work:

> On April 10, 2008, I heard the Dutch clarinetist Lars Wouters Van Den Oudenweijer at a concert on Staten Island, NY. I was blown away by the beauty of his playing and upon meeting him said, "You are one of the greatest clarinetists in the world." We bonded over refreshments at the reception and he asked me to write a piece for him. *Summer Reveries on a Mountainside* is that piece.[14]

The following excerpted exchange of emails reveals the joyful interaction between composer and performer:

10/22/08: To Lars: . . . I have already composed about 3 minutes of a solo clarinet piece. It is tonal with Richter digressions, modeled on the Bach cello suites. It will take me where it will! Every new piece is a wonderful new adventure!
08/12/09: To Lars: Your piece is 99% finished. I keep adding seasoning here and there. It has become a delicate, wistful Nocturne. I have the image of you playing it on a mountainside in a field of flowers. When I remember your playing, it is the incredible shading you bring to held, pianissimo notes that inspired me as I wrote this piece.
08/18/09: To Richter: That is wonderful news! I gratefully thank you and will do my best to bring the flowerfield to the audience!
05/09/10: To Richter: . . . I looked at your piece, and I think it is very beautiful! It will need time to grow because of its serenity. I love the idea of performing it in the festival.
11/18/10: To Lars: So, did you survive the premiere? How was it received?
11/18/10: To Richter: Yes, I survived! The audience and reviewer were very moved by your piece. It is a heavy piece, but very worth doing! Thank you so much for it.[15]

The piece was premiered and subsequently performed in the Netherlands, in Enkhuizen on November 13, 2010, and in Leiden on December 1, 2010. In a review of the premiere, critic Wouter Rulfrek described it as "a work of unsurpassed depth and intensity." Richter's *Soliloquy* for piano (2010) is a version of *Summer Reveries on a Mountainside* and explores the sonorities of the piano using various pedal effects. She premiered it at the Parrish Art Museum in Southampton, Long Island, on September 16, 2010. Several audience members described both the performance and the piece as "hypnotic."

At a December 2009 LICA concert in Cutchogue, Long Island, the Constellation Trio had performed Richter's *Divers (Diverse) Divertimento* with a substitute guitarist, Jay Sorce, of the Sorce/Lodge Duo (guitar/piano). Andrea Lodge was in the audience and the two of them asked Richter if she would write a piece for them. She agreed, and composed her twelve-minute *Serenade for Guitar and Piano* during the summer of 2010. This piece is much like her *Serenade for Flute, Percussion and Harp*: lyrical, harmonically accessible, alternating quiet passages with, sometimes Spanish-tinged, displays of virtuosity. The premiere took place at the North Shore Public Library in Wading River, Long Island, on November 5, 2010. The duo then added it to their repertoire and gave six additional performances in the 2010–11 season, including the Canadian premiere in Newfoundland. Lodge describes the work:

> Romantic in style, it features a hauntingly beautiful melody in E♭ minor over a lush, arpeggiated accompaniment. Rubati often delay phrase endings, creating heart-wrenching suspense. It feels as though one is holding one's breath, preparing to utter the next beautiful musical sentence to one's partner. The music gains urgency as block tenuto chords appear at m. 11 in the piano. The guitar is in opposition with the piano as its quintuplets react to the

piano's march-like eighth-note chords. The intensity suddenly holds off with a subito piano at m. 20. Sudden dynamic and character changes such as these are featured prominently in this music; Marga successfully keeps you on the edge of your seat! After a second major lyrical theme is introduced and developed, the music continues to build, coming to a climax with a fortissimo glissando in the piano followed by a gripping stillness. Then the secondary theme is hauntingly stated pianissimo in guitar harmonics with upper-register chords in the piano and a brief bridge leads to the original theme, now in E minor, producing a magically calming effect. Marga uses the capabilities of the two instruments skillfully, while craftily creating beautiful chamber music. We are incredibly grateful to have this beautiful gift of music from Marga. We feel a great connection to the work and have found that our audiences do also; some have stated that this piece is the most beautiful piece they have ever heard! Each time we perform it, it is met with enthusiastic, heartfelt response.[16]

In April 2011, Richter extracted the raga section of her *Landscapes of the Mind I* as a piano solo, *Raga Marwa*, and added optional percussion. This was performed by Andrea Lodge and percussionists Nick Gleason and Nick Woodbury at the Parrish Art Museum in Southampton, Long Island, on April 30, 2011.

And in June 2011, Richter wrote a short unaccompanied oboe piece, *Ode to the Grand Canyon*. The piece was inspired by a trip she had taken in May 2010 with her long-time friend Vivian Taylor to visit the Grand Canyon National Park, Zion National Park, and Bryce Canyon National Park. Rather than try to write a piece to match the vast scale of the Grand Canyon, this short piece is a quiet, hauntingly beautiful song sent aloft into the atmosphere. Terry Keevil premiered the work on October 16, 2011, in a LICA concert in Roslyn, New York, and provided in a program note his reaction to the music:

> *Ode to the Grand Canyon* is a deeply expressive work which draws upon the sustained intensity of the oboe sound. Its arching phrases eloquently convey the immensity of the Grand Canyon unencumbered by the presence of human beings. The occasional wide intervals depict the Canyon's sheer cliffs, and the slow tempo, with its measured, inevitable flow, expresses the Grand Canyon as a process, continuously in motion over eons, as the river at its heart descends and opens the earth.[17]

Also in 2011, Richter composed a five-movement suite for piano titled *Shrewsbury: Summer of 2011—Suite for Solo Piano*. About this she writes:

> It was written at my vacation retreat in the mountains of Vermont in 2011. The five pieces generally reflect the quiet, contemplative mood I often experience in that setting, although the third and fifth ones have flashes of virtuosic energy, and the overall effect is one of melancholy remembrances of things past. Embedded in pieces number 3, 4 and 5 are motifs from J. S Bach's keyboard Toccata in F♯ minor, an astonishing piece I encountered for the first time as I was composing these pieces. Knowing these specific references might enhance the

> performer's interpretation or the listeners' enjoyment, but I used them as intrinsic artistic expressions, not as a basis for flights of architectural fancy.[18]

This more tonal work, in which Richter actually uses key signatures (movements 1 and 5), is a ruminative reflection of her inner emotional life.[19]

In a recent conversation with Richter, however, her generally enthusiastic spirit certainly showed. She quipped: "I've had a wonderful life. The first eighty-five years have been really great!"

She continues to compose.

EPILOGUE

TAKING OLD AGE IN STRIDE, Richter has not thought of retiring and remains focused on composition. She continues to spend summers in Vermont and enjoys the beauty around her and visiting with professional colleagues, friends, and family. In her zest for living and her dedication to her art, Richter is a role model for younger composers and performers.

Richter's musical style has remained fairly constant throughout her life. Dissonance, slowly unfolding free forms, ostinatos and layering, a loose tonality—all of these are present in her earliest works and last throughout her compositional career. Her later works are less dissonant than her earlier ones but still use chromaticism quite freely. Richter has gone her own way, shunning any formal stylistic "schools" such as twelve-tone or neoclassicism. Her early training and selection of compositional genres reflect her Germanic roots to some degree, but mostly she exhibits an American orientation toward music in her stylistic freedom and wide-ranging selection of texts and images. She does not use Copland-like "Americanisms," though many of her works have expansive textures. The recognizable ostinato patterns and loose adherence to tonal centers make her music accessible, but the texts, slow rhythms, and dissonances also challenge the listener. Richter generates her own unique forms from her initial materials and ideas. The works are strong enough to deserve more play in the concert hall as artistic creations by a unique American woman.

While Richter dislikes the term *feminist*, she often behaves in feminist ways. Her involvement with the League of Women Composers, her participation on concerts of music by women composers, her drive, her view of her work as an important part of her individual identity, and her independence of thought all seem feminist. She has always had a confidence and belief in her own artistic skill irrespective of the external successes and reviews that she has received. Nonetheless, she also likes the traditional gender roles. She was mostly financially supported by her husband and valued being the primary caretaker of her children. The tension between the various aspects of her life makes her an intriguing figure to consider in thinking about women's roles today.

CATALOG OF COMPOSITIONS

Unless otherwise stated, Richter's compositions are available from Carl Fischer, Inc., New York. "SP" indicates works available from Shrewsbury Press. "W" indicates works that have been withdrawn by the composer for consideration.

Shrewsbury Press
45 Glen Na Little Trail
Huntington, NY 11743
Email: margarichter@optonline.net

Stage

1950 All Desire Is Sad, chamber orchestra, dance score for Juilliard. W.
1952 The Wanderers, chamber orchestra, dance score for choreographer James Waring. W.
1952 Johnny Got His Gun, chamber orchestra, dance score for choreographer Irving Burton. W.
1953 The Vagabonds, two pianos and percussion, dance score for choreographer Alec Rubin. (Also titled Miracles.) W.
1964–65 Abyss for orchestra (1-act ballet). Choreography by Stuart Hodes. Published by EMI.
1967 Bird of Yearning for orchestra (1-act ballet). Choreography by Stuart Hodes. Also concert version for small orchestra (28 players) and piano.
1995–96 Riders to the Sea (1-act chamber opera). Libretto by John Millington Synge. For soprano, mezzo-soprano, contralto, tenor, 4 or more mixed voices, flute (+ piccolo), Celtic harp/harp, accordion, tubular bells (+ bodhrán), 2 violins, viola, 2 celli.

Orchestral

1955 Concerto for Piano and Violas, Cellos and Basses. (Piano Concerto No. 1.)
1956 Lament, string orchestra. Published by Broude Brothers/Rongwen Music, 1958.
1957 Aria and Toccata for viola and string orchestra. Also version for viola and piano.

1959/rev1987 Variations on a Sarabande.
1961 Eight Pieces for Orchestra, large orchestra (version of piano work).
1967 Bird of Yearning, small orchestra (28 players) (version of ballet).
1968–74 Landscapes of the Mind I (Piano Concerto No. 2), piano, large orchestra.
1976 Country Auction, symphonic band.
1976 Blackberry Vines and Winter Fruit.
1978 Fragments (version of piano work).
1978–80 Spectral Chimes/Enshrouded Hills, three quintets (flute, oboe, clarinet, French horn, bassoon; French horn, 2 trumpets, trombone, tuba; string quartet, double bass), orchestra, 1978–80.
1981–82 Düsseldorf Concerto, flute, harp, viola, small orchestra (timpani, percussion, strings) (also chamber version).
1985 Out of Shadows and Solitude, large orchestra.
1991 Quantum Quirks of a Quick Quaint Quark.
1992 Variations and Interludes on Themes from Monteverdi and Bach (triple concerto), violin, cello, piano, large orchestra.
2004 Kyrie for String Orchestra. SP.

Chamber Music

1947/rev1974 One for Two and Two for Three, 3 trombones.
1948 Sonata for Clarinet and Piano.
1950 String Quartet No. 1. SP. W.
1952 7E for wind quintet. SP. W.
1957 Aria and Toccata for viola and piano (version of orchestral work).
1958 String Quartet No. 2.
1958 Ricercare, string quartet. Also for brass quartet (French horn, 2 trumpets, tuba), or concert band.
1961 Darkening of the Light, viola. Also version for cello, 1976.
1961 Chamber Piece for flute, oboe, clarinet, bassoon, viola, cello, and bass.
1961 Three Pieces for violin and piano. Published by Prairie Dawg Press.
1963 Suite for Violin and Piano. Published by Prairie Dawg Press.
1971 Landscapes of the Mind II, violin, piano.
1975 Pastorale, 2 oboes. Published by Prairie Dawg Press.
1979 Landscapes of the Mind III, violin, cello, piano.
1981 Sonora, 2 A-clarinets, piano.
1981–82 Düsseldorf Concerto, flute, harp, viola, ensemble (timpani, percussion, string quartet, double bass) (version of orchestral work).
1983 Exequy, oboe, clarinet, cello, piano (version of piano work). SP.
1984 Seacliff Variations, violin, viola, cello, piano. SP.
1986 Obsessions, trombone. W.
1988 Qhanri (snow mountain): Tibetan Variations for Cello and Piano.
1994 Elegy, violin/flute, piano/guitar, cello ad libitum (extract from Triple Concerto). SP.
2003 Air #2 for oboe and bassoon. SP.

2004 Air #3 for flute, oboe, and guitar. SP.
2004 Kyrie for string quintet. SP.
2005 Bye-Bye Bake Shoppe for string quartet and narrator. Text by Elisabeth Raine. SP.
2005 Divers (Diverse) Divertimento for flute (bass flute), oboe (English horn) and guitar. SP.
2006 Not Your Grandmother's Four-Hand Piece (four-hand piano; with George Cork Maul). SP.
2006 Trio for alto sax, baritone horn, and piano (also in simplified version). SP.
2006 Fandango Fantasy for piano, clarinet, violin, and cello. SP.
2007 Serenade for Flute, Percussion and Harp. SP.
2008 Two Pieces for Two Violins: Pavane and Tag for Two (for students). SP.
2009 Threnody for string trio. SP.
2010 Summer Reveries on a Mountainside for solo clarinet (version of Soliloquy). SP.
2010 Serenade for Guitar and Piano. SP.
2011 Ode to the Grand Canyon for oboe. SP.
2012 Gigue for two oboes. SP.

Choral

1951 Relations, cantata. Text by Gerd Stern. SATB and orchestra. W.
1955 Three Songs of Madness and Death. Text by John Webster. SATB. SP.
1962 Psalm 91. SATB. Published by Elkan-Vogel, 1965.
1964 Three Christmas Songs. Texts by Eugene Field, Isaac Watts, and Phillips Brooks. SSAA (children's or female chorus), 2 flutes/piano. Published by Broude Brothers, 1992.
1965 Seek Him. Text from the Book of Amos. SATB. SP.
1980 To Whom? Text by Virginia Woolf. SATB. SP.
1981 Do Not Press My Hands. Text by Gabriela Mistral. SSATTB. SP.
1982 Three Songs on Poems of Emily Dickinson. SSAA. Published by G. Schirmer, 1984.
1990 Into My Heart. Texts by Robert Frost, A. E. Housman, R. Glenn Martin, Cathleen Schurr, Maureen Skelly, and Walt Whitman. SATB, oboe, French horn, 2 trumpets, trombone, baritone horn, tuba, violin, timpani, percussion. Also version for SATB, piano 4 hands. SP.

Vocal

1941 Lullaby for Mary Howell Brinkman on birth of her son (melody only). SP.
1941 Jabberwocky. Text by Lewis Carroll. Voice, piano. SP.
1942–44 Four Songs ("Alone," "Midnight," "When I Am Not With You," and "Peace." Texts respectively by Marga Richter, James Russell Lowell, Sara Teasdale, and Marga Richter. SP.
1949 Transmutation (song cycle). Texts by Chinese poets (Ch'en Yün, Liu Sung, Hsaio Kang, Chang Chi, Po Chü I, and Anonymous). Translated by Henry Hersch Hart. Soprano, piano. SP.

1950/rev1983 Into What Unknown Chamber. Text by Phyllis Latimer. Medium voice, piano. SP.

1952 Two Chinese Songs: "The Hermit," and "Fishing Picture." Texts by Chinese poets (Li Hai-Ku and Ta Chung-Kuang). Translated by Amy Lowell. Soprano, piano. SP.

1954 She, At His Funeral. Text by Thomas Hardy. Soprano, piano. SP.

1983 Lament for Art O'Leary. Text by Eileen O'Leary. Soprano, piano. SP.

1985 Sieben Lieder. Text by Francisco Tanzer. Voice, piano. SP.

1995 Sarah do not mourn me dead. Text by Sullivan Ballou. Medium voice, piano. SP.

2000 Erin Odyssey (song cycle). Text by the composer. Medium voice, piano.

2001 Testament (song cycle). Text by Anne Morrow Lindbergh. Contralto, English horn, piano. SP.

2002 Dew-drops on a Lotus Leaf (song cycle). Text by Ryokan (translated by Jakob Fischer). Countertenor/tenor, string quartet/piano. SP.

2005 Three Songs of Celebration for flute and tenor. Text by Phyllis Latimer Roberts (for students). SP.

2006 Goat Songs (song cycle) for medium voice, piano. Text by Marcia Slatkin. SP.

2007 Sonnet 128 and Sonnet 71 for medium voice, piano. Text by William Shakespeare. SP.

2009 wild moon for tenor and piano. Text by Phyllis Latimer Roberts. SP.

Piano (Easy)

1949 Short Suite No. 1 for Young Pianists ("Angry," Melancholy," "Joyful"). Published by Leeds Music Corporation, 1954/56. SP.

1953 Nocturne for Sara Lee.

1954 Short Suite No. 2 for Young Pianists ("Raindrops," "Lullaby," "Hiccups"). Published by Leeds Music Corp., 1954/56. SP.

Piano (Intermediate)

1962 A Farewell. SP.

1968 Two Piano Pieces: "The Lost People" and "The Dancers."

1970 Four Piano Pieces: "Hugh's Piece," "Elephants and Violets," "For Something That Had Gone Before," and "Bits and Snatches" ("Bits and Snatches" requires a metal drum). SP.

Piano (Advanced/Difficult)

1944 Ballet of the Pixilated Penguins. SP.

1945 March Berserk. SP.

1945 Dream Andante. W.

1954 Sonata for Piano.

1956/rev1958 Melodrama, 2 pianos.

1960 Eight Pieces for Piano. Also version for orchestra.

1963 Fragments (also orchestral version).

1964 Variations on a Theme by Latimer, piano four-hands. SP.
1974 Short Prelude in Baroque Style (version of harpsichord work). SP.
1977 Remembrances. Published by Elkan-Vogel, 1979.
1978 Requiem.
1980 Exequy. Also version for oboe, clarinet, cello, and piano. SP.
1993 Prelude for Piano (In Memoriam) (extract from Triple Concerto). SP.
1993 Quantum Quirks of a Quick Quaint Quark (version no. 3 for piano). SP.
2003 Air #1 for piano. SP.
2004 Three Improvisations for piano. SP.
2005 Regrets. SP.
2008 Four Miniatures: Homage J. S Bach, March Berserk, Valse Melancolique, and Toccatina. SP.
2010 Soliloquy. SP.
2011 Raga Marwa (optional percussion) (extract from Landscapes of the Mind I).
2011 Shrewsbury: Summer of 2011 (suite for piano in five movements).

Arrangements

FOR TWO PIANOS

2012 Borodin's String Quartet No. 2, mvt. 3 (Notturno). Published by Piano Productions Press.

FOR FOUR PIANOS: 1952–55

Copland: Rodeo. Published by Piano Productions Press.
Humperdinck: "Dream Pantomime" from Hansel and Gretel. SP.
Khachaturian: Sabre Dance. SP.
Mussorgsky: Night on Bald Mountain and The Great Gate at Kiev. SP.
Rimsky-Korsakov: Flight of the Bumblebee. SP.
Tchaikovsky: Waltzes from Eugene Onegin, The Nutcracker, Serenade for Strings, Sleeping Beauty, and Swan Lake. SP.
Tchaikovsky: "Pas de Deux" from The Nutcracker. SP.
Tchaikovsky: "Winter Scene" from The Nutcracker. Published by Piano Productions Press.
Wagner: Ride of the Valkyries. SP.
Various dances by Arthur Benjamin, Copland, Faure, Fernandez, Hovhaness, Jacoby, Kabalevsky, Lecuona, Mussorgsky, Offenbach, Shostakovich and Weill. SP.

FOR ORCHESTRAL SUITE

1954 Weill: Mahagonny. SP.

ORGAN

1974 Variations on a Theme by Neithart von Reuenthal.

1992 Quantum Quirks of a Quick Quaint Quark (version no. 2 for organ). Published by Vivace Press.

Harpsichord

1965 Soundings.
1974 Short Prelude in Baroque Style. Also version for piano. SP.

NOTES

CHAPTER 1: *The Early Years: 1926–1951*

1. Born in 1923, Rena Sylvia died in 1996; Paul Herman lived 1929–1958.
2. Marga Richter, interview by author, May 19, 2011.
3. Ibid.
4. Marga Richter, interview by author, February 22, 2005.
5. Marga Richter, interview by author, May 19, 2011.
6. Ibid.
7. Ibid.
8. Ibid.
9. Ibid.
10. Ibid.
11. Irving Boekelheide to Marga Richter, letter March 15, 1995.
12. Marga Richter, interview by author, May 19, 2011.
13. Lenore Engdahl, taped telephone interview by author, May 1, 2008.
14. Other composers who have set "Jabberwocky" include John Duke, Lee Hoiby, Deems Taylor, and Susan Botti.
15. Marga Richter, interview by author, February 22, 2005. Her sister Rena had moved out in 1941 to study voice privately in Chicago.
16. Marga Richter, interview by author, February 22, 2005.
17. For the complete anecdote see LePage, *Women Composers, Conductors, and Musicians of the Twentieth Century*, 211.
18. In 1926 the Institute of Musical Art merged with the Juilliard Graduate School, but the name change did not come about until 1946 under new president William Schuman. See Olmstead, *Juilliard*. In the summer, Richter also attended the Juilliard Summer School (which dissolved in 1952).
19. Marga Richter to author, email September 5, 2011.
20. Ibid.
21. Marga Richter, interview by author, February 22, 2005.
22. Also in 1947, the theory and history curriculum for all Juilliard students changed from three years of "traditional approaches to teaching harmony, species counterpoint,

dictation, and sight singing" to a four-year curriculum created by Schuman and Norman Lloyd called *Literature and Materials of Music*. Two anthologies by Hardy and Fish titled *Music Literature: Homophony* and *Music Literature: Polyphony* were used, remaining in print until 1995. In 1948 composer Vivian Fine taught *Literature and Materials of Music* as an adjunct. Olmstead, *Juilliard*, 150, 160–65, 275–76.

23. Marga Richter, interview by author, February 22, 2005.

24. Marga Richter, quoted in LePage, *Women Composers, Conductors, and Musicians of the Twentieth Century*, 212.

25. Persichetti, *Twentieth Century Harmony*, 13, 277.

26. Marga Richter quoted in Lee, "Marga Richter," 6.

27. Marga Richter, interview by author, May 19, 2011.

28. Marga Richter, interview by author, February 22, 2005.

29. Marga Richter, interview by author, May 19, 2011.

30. Marga Richter, interview by author, February 22, 2005.

31. Marga Richter, interview by author, May 19, 2011.

32. Ibid.

33. Ibid.

34. Ibid.

35. Phyllis Latimer later married and became Phyllis Latimer Roberts.

36. Phyllis Latimer Roberts, taped telephone interview by author, June 2, 2010.

37. The McMillan Theatre has since been renovated and renamed the Miller Theatre.

38. Peggy Glanville-Hicks, "Composers Forum," *New York Herald Tribune*, February 4, 1951, quoted in LePage, *Women Composers, Conductors, and Musicians of the Twentieth Century*, 213. The performers were clarinetist Herbert Tichman, singer Phyllis Goodmund, and pianist Marga Richter.

39. Harman, "Forum Hears Music by Richter, Sokoloff."

40. Marga Richter, interview by author, February 22, 2005.

41. Ibid.

42. Ibid.

43. Marga Richter, interview by author, May 3, 2005.

44. Marga Richter, interview by author, May 19, 2011.

45. Richter has long enjoyed a daily shot of scotch in the afternoon, and an occasional Guinness beer or glass of wine. Perhaps this alcohol consumption, a change from the social norms of her midwestern and Christian Science upbringing, helped support a feeling of camaraderie with other professional musicians. (Her second husband Skelly only drank alcohol occasionally at a party.) For an overview of the sometimes conflicting research on the extra stigma for women who use or are addicted to alcohol, and the underreporting of women's alcohol use versus the convergence hypothesis due to changing sex roles, see Babcock, "Does Feminism Drive Women to Drink?" For a brief overview of the differing attitudes of first-, second-, and third-wave feminists toward women drinking, see Ehrenreich, "Libation as Liberation?"

46. Marga Richter, taped interview by author, June 13–14, 2006.

CHAPTER 2: *Modern Dance and the MGM Recordings: 1951–1960*

1. Marga Richter, interview by author, February 22, 2005.

2. Ibid.

3. Marga Richter, interview by author, May 24, 2011.

4. Olsen was the wife of Arthur Winograd, cellist, and a founding member of the Juilliard Quartet.

5. Marga Richter, interview by author, May 24, 2011. The cause of the fire was never determined.

6. Marga Richter, interview by author, February 22, 2005.

7. Born in 1925, octogenarian Burton was still dancing in Bergenfield, N.J., in 2005.

8. Marga Richter, interview by author, February 22, 2005.

9. In 1962, Rubin would found an experimental dance and theater company originally called the Theatre of Encounter, which was renamed the Theatre Within. Rubin became known as a maverick director and therapist, and many famous people worked at the Theatre Within, including Al Pacino.

10. Marga Richter, interview by author, February 22, 2005.

11. The Lortel Archives has records of Lenya in *The Threepenny Opera* from March 10 to May 30, 1954, and also from September 20, 1955, to December 17, 1961. At the time the Lortel Theater was called the Theatre De Lys. See the Lortel Archives: The Internet Off-Broadway Database, http://www.lortel.org/lla_archive/ (accessed June 4, 2010). Also see the Kurt Weil Foundation for Music, http://www.kwf.org/kwf/detailed-chronology-1950–1959 (accessed June 4, 2010).

12. Over fifty years later, in 2008, Richter was paid $8,500 from the Kurt Weill Foundation for a photo she had along with two pages of music manuscript by Kurt Weill and a few pages of the score of *The Threepenny Opera*.

13. Michael now teaches piano at Columbia University, and Maureen is an obstetrics nurse in Upstate New York.

14. Marga Richter, quoted in LePage, *Women Composers, Conductors, and Musicians of the Twentieth Century*, 214.

15. Marga Richter, interview by author, February 22, 2005.

16. Dianne Goolkasian Rahbee to Michael Slayton, letter 2006. My thanks to Michael Slayton for sharing this with me.

17. Marga Richter, interview by author, February 22, 2005.

18. Ibid.

19. Maureen Raj, taped telephone interview by author, April 19, 2008.

20. Marga Richter, interview by author, February 22, 2005.

21. Richter was also the pianist for MGM recordings of two Surinach piano pieces (E3419) and three Hovhaness piano pieces (E3517).

22. Hinson, *Guide to the Pianist's Repertoire*, 643.

23. See Burge, "Aaron Copland, Roger Sessions, and the Mid-Century Piano Sonata."

24. For a detailed structural analysis of the Sonata using set theory, see You Ju Lee, "Marga Richter," 50–80. Alan Gregory also provides a brief analysis of the Sonata in the liner notes for Peter Basquin's Grenadilla recording: Grenadilla Records GS 1010, 1978.

25. Celliot Zucherman, *American Record Guide*, 1956, quoted in LePage, *Women Composers, Conductors, and Musicians of the Twentieth Century*, 203.

26. Alfred Frankenstein, *High Fidelity*, December 1956, 90, quoted in Lee, "Marga Richter," 8.

27. Hall Overton, *Metronome*, December 1956, 42, quoted in Lee, "Marga Richter," 9.

28. John Rosenfield, review of Menahem Pressler recording, MR collection.

29. E. S. V. Leigh, *New Records*, February 1979, MR collection.

30. Arthur Cohn, *Recorded Classical Music: A Critical Guide to Compositions and Performances* (New York: Collier Macmillan, 1981), 1504, quoted in Lee, "Marga Richter," 13.

31. Davis, "Long Island Composers' Alliance Presents Works of Five Members."

32. Barnaby Miln, "Performance in Wigmore Hall," *London Daily Telegraph*, May 2, 1981.

33. Radu A. Lelutiu, *Fanfare Magazine*, March 2012.

34. Michael Redmond, interview by author, October 13, 2009.

35. Sterne, review of *Concerto for Piano, Violas, Celli and Basses*.

36. Frankenstein, "Premiere by Little Symphony."

37. Oliver Daniel, *Saturday Review*, December 26, 1959, quoted in LePage, *Women Composers, Conductors, and Musicians of the Twentieth Century*, 214.

38. Unsigned review, *Long Player*, May 1958, quoted in Ammer, *Unsung*, 213.

39. Miller, review of *Richter*.

40. Marga Richter, interview by author, May 24, 2011.

41. Ainslee Cox conducted the American Composers Orchestra and the Riverside Symphony during the 1980s in New York City, in addition to the Goldman Concert Band. He was educated at Westminster Choir College in Princeton, N.J., and at the University of Texas at Austin.

42. Nancy Gilson, *Oklahoma Journal*, January 12, 1976, quoted in LePage, *Women Composers, Conductors, and Musicians of the Twentieth Century*, 221.

43. Arthur Cohn to Marga Richter, letter April 26, 1988.

44. Frankenstein, review of *M-G-M Records Presents Marga Richter*.

45. *Metronome*, December 1956, 42, quoted in Lee, "Marga Richter," 9.

46. Marga Richter, videotaped interview by Frances Harmeyer, July 9, 1975, interview no. 51 a–e, transcript, Oral History of American Music, Yale University, New Haven, Conn., 88–89.

47. Numerous favorable reviews followed, including John Harvey, "'Lament' Triggers Longing for Contemporary Richter"; Roy M. Close, review of Minnesota Orchestra Concert; and Michael Anthony, "Orchestra Plays Composer's 'Lament.'"

48. Marga Richter, interview by author, May 24, 2011.

49. Quoted in Zakariasen, "Jerseyans Feature New Work by Women" (Zakariasen errs in his review by stating that the work was dedicated to Samuel Barber).

50. *Journeys: Orchestral Works by American Women*, CD, Leonarda LE 327, 1987.

51. Kenneth LaFave, *Kansas City Star*, July 31, 1988, 4D, quoted in Lee, "Marga Richter," 9.

52. Sterne, review of *Concerto for Piano, Violas, Celli and Basses* and *Aria and Toccata*.

53. Ed Cole, LP liner notes to *M-G-M Records Presents Marga Richter: Aria and Toccata*, E3559.

54. "The Spotlight," *Parkersburg (W.V.) News*, August 1, 1954.

55. *Players Magazine*, March 1955.

56. Jack Kilpatrick, "Little Treasures," *Clearwater Sun*, February 6, 1955, 5.

57. "Record Reviews," *Miami Daily News*, June 26, 1955.

58. Francis Klein, "Concert Notes," *St. Louis Globe-Democrat*, July 31, 1955, 5F.

59. *Nocturne for Sara Lee*, along with two later works: *The Dancers* and *The Lost People*, was published in 2001 by Carl Fischer in volume 2 of the Masters of Our Day series, *Twenty-two New Works Written Specially for Young Pianists by Some of Today's Most Important American Composers*. The collection also includes compositions by Norman Dello Joio, David Del Tredici, Lukas Foss, and Ned Rorem.

60. Jessye Norman to Marga Richter, letter February 25, 1977.

61. Marga Richter, "Note" preface to the score of *Melodrama*.

62. Ibid.

63. Michael Skelly, taped telephone interview by author, March 19, 2008.

64. You Ju Lee, "Marga Richter," 20–21, shows similarity between the *String Quartet No. 2*, mm. 8–10, and Shostakovich's *Concerto in C Minor*, op. 35., 2nd mvt., mm. 129–132, pointing out the half-step motion and the widely spaced sonorities.

65. *Southampton Press*, March 22, 1973, quoted in Lee, "Marga Richter," 10.

66. Simon, "Philharmonic to Spotlight Five Composers."

67. Marga Richter, liner notes for *Diverse Light*, CD, Capstone Records CPS-8692, 2001.

68. Marga Richter, interview by author, May 24, 2011.

69. Richter, program note for *Variations on a Sarabande*.

70. Sherman, "Civic Orchestra Displays Increasing Sophistication."

CHAPTER 3: *Fragments: 1960s*

1. In 1964, composer Vivian Fine would begin teaching part-time at Bennington College.

2. Marga Richter, interview by author, February 23, 2005. The MacDowell Colony, near Peterborough, N.H., and Yaddo, in Saratoga Springs, N.Y., are both artists' communities.

3. Marga Richter, interview by author, February 23, 2005.

4. Hinson, *Guide to the Pianist's Repertoire*, 643.

5. Marga Richter, interview by Frances Harmeyer, 51.

6. Russell Bliss, *Long Islander*, MR collection.

7. *I Ching: Hexagram No. 36*, cited in preface to the score of *Darkening of the Light*.

8. Richter, "Notes for *Soundings*."

9. Richter, program note for *Soundings*.

10. Libbey, "Review of Sunday Concert."

11. Marga Richter, interview by author, May 24, 2011.

12. Robert Lee Tipps, *Long Islander*, April 18, 1964, MR collection.

13. Marga Richter, interview by author, February 22, 2005.

14. Ibid.

15. Fried, "Four Numbers, One Standout."

16. Marga Richter to Clive Barnes, letter February 3, 1967.
17. Barnes, "Modern Dance"; Barnes, "Ballet: Hodes's 'Abyss'"; Barnes, "Ballet: Joffrey's 'Petrushka,' 'Abyss.'"
18. Wagner, "Symphony Salutes Prager in One of Best Concerts This Season."
19. Ernestine Stodelle, *New Haven Register*, 1982, MR collection.
20. Marga Richter, interview by author, February 23, 2005.
21. Marga Richter to author, email May 28, 2011.

CHAPTER 4: *Landscapes: 1970s*

1. Marga Richter to author, email April 5, 2012.
2. Under Skrowaczewski, the Minneapolis Symphony Orchestra was renamed the Minnesota Orchestra in 1968.
3. Marga Richter to author, email June 5, 2011.
4. Marga Richter, interview by Frances Harmeyer, 28.
5. Ibid., 29.
6. Ibid., 31.
7. Foulkes-Levy and Levy, *Journeys through the Life and Music of Nancy Van de Vate*.
8. The IAWM also cosponsored the journal *Women and Music: A Journal of Gender and Culture* from 1997 to 2008.
9. For more information on Leonarda, visit its Web site at www.leonarda.com.
10. Marnie Hall, phone interview by author, February 21, 2008.
11. Ibid.
12. Marga Richter, quoted in LePage, *Women Composers, Conductors, and Musicians of the Twentieth Century*, 222–23.
13. Putnam, "Women in Music."
14. Robert Friou to Thomas Putnam, letter September 20, 1986.
15. Marga Richter, interview by author, February 23, 2005.
16. Ibid.
17. Hughes, "Composers Series Opens at Modern."
18. Johnson, "Marga Richter."
19. Tom Johnson to Marga Richter, letter September 18, 1975.
20. Marga Richter to Tom Johnson, letter September 22, 1975.
21. Michael Anthony, *Minneapolis Tribune*, October 22, 1976, quoted in LePage, *Women Composers, Conductors, and Musicians of the Twentieth Century*, 208.
22. John Harvey, *St. Paul Dispatch and Pioneer Press*, October 25, 1976, quoted in LePage, *Women Composers, Conductors, and Musicians of the Twentieth Century*, 208.
23. Marga Richter, CD liner notes to *Snow Mountain: A Spiritual Trilogy*, Leonarda LE 337, 1994.
24. The cloud-bone analogy is from Marga Richter, interview by author, February 23, 2005.
25. Richter, program note for *Landscapes of the Mind I*.
26. Marga Richter, interview by author, June 7, 2011.
27. Marga Richter, quoted in LePage, *Women Composers, Conductors, and Musicians of the Twentieth Century*, 215–16.

28. Richter frequently notates the D♭ enharmonically as C♯ in the work.

29. Marga Richter, interview by author, June 7, 2011.

30. Georgia O'Keeffe to Richter, letter, May 19, 1974, MR's personal correspondence.

31. In 1975 Michael Tilson Thomas had recommended Richter's *Landscapes of the Mind I* for a reading of new compositions with the Buffalo Symphony with Richter as soloist.

32. Cheek, "Symphony's 'Landscapes' a Real Triumph."

33. LaFave, "'Landscapes' Premiere Shows Vital Musical Ideas."

34. Uhrig, "Richter 'Landscapes of the Mind' Gets Cool Reception at Music Hall."

35. Cherry, review of Tucson Symphony Orchestra Concert, and "Tucson Sym."

36. Hinderas (1927–1987) was a U.S. concert pianist who often promoted and recorded works by black composers.

37. Hinely, "Report on the Fourth International Congress on Women in Music," 5.

38. Henry, "Composer Richter Blends Ideas of Art, Music."

39. Henry, "Atlanta Symphony."

40. Marga Richter to Daniel Heifetz, letter October 13, 1971.

41. Marga Richter, interview by author, May 3, 2005.

42. Allen Hughes, *New York Times*, May 1, 1977, quoted in LePage, *Women Composers, Conductors, and Musicians of the Twentieth Century*, 219.

43. Cohn, *Literature of Chamber Music*, 2303; the remaining quotations are from Carl Fischer, press release, 1979, MR collection.

44. Richter, "Program Note *Landscapes of the Mind II*."

45. Marga Richter, interview by author, May 3, 2005.

46. Richter, "Program Note *Landscapes of the Mind III*."

47. Heuwell Tircuit, "The People Behind the Music," *San Francisco Chronicle*, May 6, 1979.

48. Bob Micklin, *Newsday*, June 9, 1979, MR collection.

49. Battisti, *Winds of Change*, 200.

50. Marga Richter, interview by author, March 17, 2011.

51. Byron Belt, *Long Island Press*, July 12, 1976, MR collection.

52. Henry David Thoreau and Eliot Porter, *In Wildness Is the Preservation of the World*. Text by Thoreau, photographs by Porter (New York: Sierra Club, 1962/1967), 5.

53. Ibid. Richter omitted the words "in sunny places look" from her liner notes to the CD recording of *Blackberry Vines and Winter Fruit*.

54. Thoreau and Porter, *In Wildness Is the Preservation of the World*, 106–7, 22–23. In her CD liner notes of *Blackberry Vines and Winter Fruit*, after "retain their color throughout," Richter added the words "the winter, and appear more brilliantly than ever the succeeding spring."

55. Lawrence B. Johnson, *High Fidelity/Musical America*, September 1977, MR collection.

56. Marga Richter, CD liner notes to *The London Philharmonic Celebrates American Composers*, Leonarda LE 331, 1990.

57. Walsh, "Young Conductor with Two Styles."

58. Commanday, "Triumphant Night for the Oakland Symphony."

59. Hertelendy, "Conductor Calvin Simmons."

60. Hughes, "Concert."

61. Wayne, "Berkshire Symphony in Finale."

62. Ellis, "Want List 1991."

63. Bob Doerschuk, "Sheet Music," *Contemporary Keyboard* (April 1981): 58. The work is also described and categorized as "M–D" (Medium–Difficult) in Hinson, *Guide to the Pianist's Repertoire*, 643.

64. Marga Richter, CD liner notes to *Snow Mountain: A Spiritual Trilogy*, Leonarda LE 337, 1994, 2–3.

65. Lee, "Marga Richter," 45–49, provides a detailed analysis.

66. Hinson, *Guide to the Pianist's Repertoire*, 643.

67. Sorrel Hays to author, email June 12, 2008.

68. Ibid. Richter had met Reichbach at the Sea Cliff Chamber Players premiere of her *Seacliff Variations*. Reichbach named the painting *Blackberry Vines* because while painting the portrait, Reichbach played a recording of Richter's *Blackberry Vines and Winter Fruit*, thus capturing the reactions of both Reichbach and Richter to the music. After Roberta Reichbach died, the painting went to her sister Naomi Reichbach. Naomi is now deceased, and the painting is with Naomi's partner, Margot Hagaman, in Albany, New York.

69. Byron Belt, "Women's Music Program a Hit for Best Reasons," *Jersey Journal* (March 19, 1979), 11.

70. Allan Kozinn, *Charleston News & Courier—The Evening Post*, 1981, MR collection.

71. Eva-Elizabeth Fischer, *Süddeutsche Zeitung*, 1984, MR collection.

72. LePage, *Women Composers, Conductors, and Musicians of the Twentieth Century*, 223–24.

73. Lorraine, "Recovering Jouissance," 8, 14–16.

CHAPTER 5: *Expansion: 1980s*

1. In LePage, *Women Composers, Conductors, and Musicians of the Twentieth Century*, the work is identified as *Concerto for Three Quintets and Orchestra*.

2. Marga Richter, "Performance Note Music for *Three Quintets and Orchestra*," unpublished typescript photocopy, MR collection.

3. Mark Lehman, CD liner notes to *Modern American Classics, Volume 3*, MMC 2066, 1998, 2.

4. Ibid., 3–4.

5. See Court, review of *Modern American Classics, Volume 3*.

6. Denton, review of *Modern American Classics, Volume 3*.

7. Garland, remarks on *Evening Music*.

8. An exequy is a funeral rite or procession.

9. Marga Richter to author, email June 28, 2011.

10. Henry King (1592–1669) was an English poet who eventually became the bishop of Chichester. King wrote many elegies on royal persons and on his private friends.

11. Richter, "Notes to *Lament for Art O'Leary*."

12. Virginia Woolf, *The Waves* (New York: Harcourt, Brace, 1931), 56–57. The passage appears in Rhoda's monologue after her "Empress dream" and beginning "I will go now into the library and take out some book, and read and look; and read again and look."

13. John Rockwell, "Music: Calliope Singers," *New York Times*, March 8, 1981, 49.

14. Melba Cuddy-Keane, "Virginia Woolf, Sound Technologies, and the New Aurality,"

in *Virginia Woolf in the Age of Mechanical Reproduction*, ed. Pamela L. Caughie (New York: Garland, 2000), 94, 87, 87–90.

15. Susan Dick, "Literary Realism in *Mrs. Dalloway*, *To the Lighthouse*, *Orlando* and *The Waves*," in *The Cambridge Companion to Virginia Woolf*, ed. Sue Roe and Susan Sellars (Cambridge: Cambridge Univ. Press, 2000), 66–71.

16. Emily Dalgarno discusses this passage and the preceding one, in which Rhoda fantasizes about being a Russian Empress, in the context of imperialist ideology. See Dalgarno, "Solar Light and Darkness: 'The Waves,'" in *Virginia Woolf and the Visible World* (Cambridge: Cambridge Univ. Press, 2001), 107.

17. See Janet Goldman, *The Feminist Aesthetics of Virginia Woolf: Modernism, Post-Impressionism and the Politics of the Visual* (Cambridge: Cambridge Univ. Press, 1998), 195; and Thomas C. Caramagno, "'I Do Not Know Altogether Who I Am': The Plurality of Intrasubjective Life in *The Waves*," in *The Flight of the Mind: Virginia Woolf's Art and Manic-Depressive Illness* (Berkeley: Univ. of California Press, 1992), 278–79.

18. R. W. Franklin, ed., *The Poems of Emily Dickinson*, variorum ed., vol. 1 (Cambridge, Mass.: Belknap Press of Harvard University Press, 1998).

19. Marga Richter to author, email June 28, 2011. Also in earlier form in Lee, "Marga Richter," 14.

20. *Fanfare*, 1985; Robert Croan, *Pittsburgh Post-Gazette*, Sept. 27, 1985, MR collection.

21. Libbey, review of Sunday concert.

22. "Chronik," *Düsseldorfer Stadtpost/Düsseldorfer Feuilleton*, October 30, 1981.

23. Richter, "Program Note: *Düsseldorf Concerto*."

24. Milbouer, "Composer Draws on Roots in Writing Concerto."

25. Kosman, "Pioneer Theme for Philharmonic."

26. Hertelendy, "'Ghosts' Was Only Chance for Women's Philharmonic."

27. DePinto, "Women's Philharmonic Premieres Three Works."

28. JoAnn Falletta to author, email March 19, 2009.

29. "Marga Richter's *Sieben Lieder*."

30. Steven L. Rosenhaus, *Musical Heritage Review* 14, no. 9, 1990, MR collection.

31. Marga Richter, program note for *Seacliff Variations*, MR collection.

32. For a detailed analysis of *Qhanri*, see Mirchandani, "Marga Richter."

33. Marga Richter, CD liner notes to *Snow Mountain: A Spiritual Trilogy*, Leonarda LE 337, 1994, 2.

34. Michael Redmond, "Recordings," *(Newark) Star-Ledger*, May 26, 1995, MR collection.

35. Jocelyn Mackey, *Pan Pipes*, summer 1997, quoted in Ammer, *Unsung*, 214.

36. *Friends of Music at Guilford Presents David Wells*, Feb. 9, 2007, http://ibrattleboro.com/ (accessed May 28, 2009).

37. *Out of Shadows and Solitude* was originally titled "Symphony No. 1."

38. Marga Richter, interview by author, March 17, 2011.

39. Marga Richter, program note for *Out of Shadows and Solitude*, MR collection.

40. Peter Bates, CD liner notes to *Richter, Burwasser, Theurer, Moyer, Bullen, Harris*, MMC Recordings MMC2118, 2003, 1.

41. Marga Richter to author, email November 13, 2011.

CHAPTER 6: *Culmination: 1990s*

1. Goodman, "Quintets of Quick Quips, Quintessentially Quirky."
2. Richter, program note to *Quantum Quirks of a Quick Quaint Quark*.
3. Mark Lehman, CD liner notes to *Modern American Classics, Vol. 3*, MMC 2066, 1998.
4. Denton, review of *Modern American Classics, Volume 3*.
5. Sheldon Morgenstern to Richter, letter April 27, 1993.
6. Jones, "Faculty Trio Performs Story of Faith Found."
7. Richter, program note for *Variations and Interludes on Themes from Monteverdi and Bach*, draft dated September 26, 2002, MR collection.
8. Richter, program note to *Variations and Interludes on Themes from Monteverdi and Bach*, 2011.
9. Robert Lee Tipps to Richter, letter June 21, 2002.
10. Murray Cohen to Richter, email April 28, 2004.
11. Barbara Kupferberg to Richter, letter June 5, 1993.
12. Marga Richter, interview by author, March 17, 2011.
13. Goodman, "L. I. Composer's Opera Finally Arrives."
14. Hanging on her living room wall, Richter keeps as decoration five bells that she used in the performance. They were made by Tom Torrens from oxygen tanks and are tuned to the pitches A, B flat, B natural, C, and C.
15. Goodman, "L. I. Composer's Opera Finally Arrives."
16. Angela Malek to author, email February 16, 2010.
17. Although the original letter is lost, several versions exist. Richter's source was a column discussing the Ken Burns film on the Civil War: Anna Quindlen, "Public and Private; Moving Pictures," *New York Times*, September 27, 1990, A23.
18. Marga Richter, taped telephone interview by Bruce Duffie, July 18, 1996.
19. Marga Richter, interview by You Ju Lee, December 28, 1998, quoted in Lee, "Marga Richter," 19.

CHAPTER 7: *Blooming: 2000s–Present*

1. Earlier pieces written in response to intense personal involvements include: *Sonata for Piano*, *Aria and Toccata*, *Darkening of the Light*, *Remembrances*, and *Requiem*.
2. Marga Richter, *Erin Odyssey* (New York: Carl Fischer, 2000).
3. Marga Richter, *Bye-Bye Bake Shoppe, Text by Elisabeth Raine* (Shrewsbury Press, 2005).
4. Marga Richter, interview by author, March 17, 2011.
5. Richter, program note for *Divers (Diverse) Divertimento*.
6. Marga Richter, interview by author, March 17, 2011.
7. Richter, program note for *Sonnet 128* and *Sonnet 71*.
8. Michael Skelly, taped telephone interview by author, March 19, 2008.
9. Marga Richter, interview by author, March 17, 2011.
10. Marga Richter to author, email June 10, 2011.
11. Richter, program note for *Fandango Fantasy*.
12. Rebecca Patterson to author, email March 16, 2010.
13. Marga Richter to author, email June 10, 2011.

14. Marga Richter to author, email October 9, 2011.

15. Ibid.

16. Andrea Lodge to author, email November 10, 2011.

17. Terry Keevil, program note for *Ode to the Grand Canyon*, MR collection.

18. Marga Richter to author, email October 3, 2011. The Bach motifs are from the moderato, mm. 109 and 131, and the fugue, mm. 136–37.

19. The harmonic layout of the movements in the suite are as follows: 1. (key sig.) F♯ minor; 2. Begins in D min., ends in E min.; 3. Begins in E maj./min., ends in prolonged E min., but last chord is A min.; 4. Begins in F♯ min., ends in F min.; 5. (key sig.) F♯ min., begins and ends in F♯ min.; So: F♯–D–E–A–F♯–F♮–F♯.

DISCOGRAPHY

Selected Performances on CD from Marga Richter's Personal Collection

Dew-drops on a Lotus Leaf (song cycle). Text by Ryokan (translated by Jakob Fischer). William George, countertenor with the Long Island String Quartet.
Fandango Fantasy. Antares Piano-Clarinet Quartet.
Relations cantata
  Excerpts from rehearsal. WNYC interview 3/25/53.
  National Orchestra Association; Leon Barzin, conductor.
Sarah do not mourn me dead. William George, tenor; Mitchell Kirker, piano.
Seacliff Variations. Sea Cliff Chamber Players.
Serenade for Guitar and Piano. Sorce/Lodge Duo (Jay Sorce, guitar; Andrea Lodge, piano).
Sonata for Clarinet and Piano
  Herbert Tichman, clarinet; Marga Richter, piano.
  Mariko Sudo, clarinet; Maria Salabasheva, piano.
  Naomi Drucker, clarinet; Marga Richter, piano.
Soliloquy. Marga Richter, piano.
Summer Reveries on a Mountainside. Lars Wouters Van Den Oudenweijer, clarinet.
Threnody for string trio. American Chamber Ensemble.
Variations on a Theme by Neithart von Reuenthal. Leonard Raver, organ.
LICA Concert
  Air #1 for piano
  Three Improvisations for piano
  Marga Richter, piano
Smithtown Recital
  Jabberwocky
  Prelude for Piano
  Testament
  Air #1
  Erin Odyssey
  Terry Keevil, English horn; Melissa Maravell, contralto and guitar; Marga Richter, piano.

Selected Performances of Choral Works on Cassette Tape from Marga Richter's Personal Collection

Do Not Press My Hands. SSATTB (6:00). Western Wind.
Into My Heart. SATB (18:15). New Amsterdam Singers, with Chamber Ensemble. Clara Longstreth, conductor.
Into My Heart. SATB (18:15). Georgia State University, with Piano Four-Hands.
Psalm 91. SATB (3:30). Nassau Community College Choir.
Seek Him. SATB (4:30). Nassau Community College Choir.
Three Songs of Madness and Death. SATB (6:40). Occasional Singers.
To Whom? SATB (6:20). New Calliope Singers.

Commercially Available CDs

Character Sketches: Solo Piano Works by 7 American Women.
Nanette Kaplan Solomon, piano. Leonarda: LE 334, 1994.
Exequy
Fragments
Diverse Light
Meridian String Quartet. Capstone: CPS-8692, 2001.
String Quartet No. 2
Journeys: Orchestral Works by American Women
Carolann Martin/Bournemouth Sinfonietta. Leonarda: LE 327, 1987.
Lament
The London Philharmonic Celebrates American Composers
Harold Farberman/London Philharmonic. Leonarda: LE 331, 1990.
Blackberry Vines and Winter Fruit
Modern American Classics, Volume 3
Gerard Schwarz/Czech Radio Symphony Orchestra. MMC: 2066, 1998.
Spectral Chimes/Enshrouded Hills
Quantum Quirks of a Quick Quaint Quark
Orchestral Excursions
Renata Knific, violin; Pamela Frame, cello; Robert Weirich, piano; Joel Suben/Polish Radio National Symphony Orchestra. Leonarda: LE 351, 2004.
Variations and Interludes on Themes from Monteverdi and Bach
Persichetti and Pupils: Piano Music of Vincent Persichetti, Marga Richter, and Jacob Druckman
Richard Zimdars, piano. Albany Troy 1310, 2011.
Eight Pieces for Piano
Remembrances
Sonata for Piano
Riders to the Sea/Kyrie
Conductor: Daijiro Ukon. Soloists: Susan Holsonbake, soprano; Anna Tonna, mezzo-soprano; Melissa Maravell, contralto; Aram Tchobanian, tenor.
Riders to the Sea

Motyl String Quartet; Pawel Knapik, double bass.
Kyrie
Leonarda: LE358 CD, 2011.

Seacliff Variations
Sea Cliff Chamber Players. Musical Heritage Society: MHS 5512563L.
Seacliff Variations

Seattle Symphony Orchestra
Gerard Schwarz/Seattle Symphony Orchestra. MMC: 2118, 2003.
Out of Shadows and Solitude

Snow Mountain: A Spiritual Trilogy
David Wells, cello and Marga Richter, piano.
Qhanri
Marga Richter, piano.
Requiem
Daniel Heifetz, violin and Michael Skelly, piano.
Landscapes of the Mind II
Leonarda: LE 337, 1994.

Women Composers for Organ-Music Spanning Five Centuries
Barbara Harbach, organ. Gasparo: GSCD 294, 2006.
Quantum Quirks of a Quick Quaint Quark No. 2

LP Recordings

Clarinet Violin Piano
Daniel Heifetz, violin; Michael Skelly, piano.
Landscapes of the Mind II
The Drucker Trio: Stanley Drucker, clarinet; Naomi Drucker, clarinet; Blanche Abram, piano. Liner notes by Melvin Berger. *Sonora* Leonarda LPI 122, 1984.

Michael Colgrass and Marga Richter
Peter Basquin, piano. Liner notes by Alan Gregory. Grenadilla Records GS 1010, 1978.
Sonata for Piano

M-G-M Records. *Tchaikovsky Waltzes* transcribed for 4 pianos.
Manhattan Piano Quartet. E3100.

M-G-M Records. *Concert Favorites* transcribed for 4 pianos.
Manhattan Piano Quartet. E3130.

M-G-M Records Presents Piano Music for Children by Modern American Composers
Marga Richter, piano. E3147.
Two Short Suites for Young Pianists

M-G-M Records Presents Piano Music for Children by Modern Composers
Marga Richter, piano. E3181.

M-G-M Records. *Dances* transcribed for 4 pianos.
Manhattan Piano Quartet. E3224.

M-G-M Records Presents Marga Richter: Sonata for Piano
Menahem Pressler, piano. E3244.
Sonata for Piano

M-G-M Records Presents Marga Richter: Lament for Strings
Izler Solomon conducting the M-G-M String Orchestra. E3422.
Lament

M-G-M Records Presents Marga Richter: Transmutation and Other Songs
Dorothy Renzi, soprano, with Maro Ajemian, piano. E3546.
The Hermit
Fishing Picture
Transmutation

M-G-M Records Presents Marga Richter: Concerto for Piano and Violas, Cellos and Basses
William Masselos, piano; Carlos Surinach/M-G-M String Orchestra. E3547.
Concerto for Piano, Violas, Cellos and Basses

M-G-M Records Presents Marga Richter: Aria and Toccata
Walter Trampler, viola; Carlos Surinach/M-G-M String Orchestra. E3559.
Aria and Toccata

BIBLIOGRAPHY

Materials Privately Held by Marga Richter, Including Manuscript Scores

SELECTED LETTERS

Irving Boekelheide to Richter, March 15, 1995.
Ed Cole to Richter, September 23, 1981.
Robert Friou to Thomas Putnam, September 20, 1986.
Tom Johnson to Richter, September 18 and 27, 1975.
Barbara Kupferberg to Richter, June 5, 1993.
Phyllis Latimer Roberts to author, January 21, 2011.
Sheldon Morgenstern to Richter, April 27, 1993.
Georgia O'Keeffe to Richter, May 19, 1974.
Dianne Goolkasian Rahbee to Michael Slayton, 2006.
Marga Richter to Clive Barnes, February 3, 1967.
Marga Richter to Daniel Heifetz, October 13, 1971.
Marga Richter to Tom Johnson, September 22, 1975.
Marga Richter to Georgia O'Keeffe, 1974.
Stanislaw Skrowaczewski to Richter, January 8, 1980.
Stanislaw Skrowaczewski to Richter, January 6, 1981?.
Stanislaw Skrowaczewski to Richter, March 5, 2004?.
Stanislaw Skrowaczewski to Richter, August 23, 2007.
Robert Lee Tipps to Richter, June 21, 2002.

SELECTED EMAIL MESSAGES

Murray Cohen to Marga Richter, April 28, 2004.
JoAnn Falletta to author, March 19, 2009.
Sorrel Hays to author, Thursday, June 12, 2008.
Angela Malek to author, February 16, 2010.
Rebecca Patterson to author, March 16, 2010.
Paul Rapoport to Marga Richter, September 22, 2010.
Michael Redmond to Marga Richter, October 5, 2009.

SELECTED PROGRAM NOTES

Marga Richter. Program note for *Landscapes of the Mind I.*
Marga Richter. "[Analysis of] *Landscapes of the Mind II.*" April 13, 1975. Photocopy.
Marga Richter. "Program Note *Landscapes of the Mind III.*" Unpublished typescript photocopy.
Marga Richter. *Manifesto 2010*, unpublished typescript.
Marga Richter. "Notes to *Lament for Art O'Leary.*" Unpublished typescript photocopy.
Marga Richter. "Notes for *Soundings.*" Unpublished typescript photocopy.
Marga Richter. "Performance Note: *Music for Three Quintets and Orchestra*," Unpublished typescript photocopy.
Marga Richter. "Program Note: *Düsseldorf Concerto*," New Hampshire Music Festival, summer 1987 (shorter version in score).
Marga Richter. Program note for *Divers (Diverse) Divertimento.*
Marga Richter. Program note for *Fandango Fantasy.*
Marga Richter. Program note for *Kyrie* for strings.
Marga Richter. Program note for *Sonnet 128* and *Sonnet 71.*
Marga Richter. Program note for *Quantum Quirks of a Quick Quaint Quark.*
Marga Richter. Program note for *Soundings*. October 18, 1981.
Marga Richter. Program note for *Variations on a Sarabande.* Photocopy.
Marga Richter. Program note for *Variations and Interludes on Themes from Monteverdi and Bach*. Draft dated September 26, 2002; note in *Orchestral Excursions* CD. Leonarda: LE 351, 2004; revised copy, July 8, 2011.

INTERVIEWS

Marga Richter, interview by author, May 3, 2005.
Lenore Engdahl, taped telephone interview by author, May 1, 2008.
Marnie Hall, taped telephone interview by author, February 21, 2008.
Maureen Raj, taped telephone interview by author, April 19, 2008.
Michael Redmond, telephone interview by author, October 13, 2009.
Marga Richter, taped interview by Frances Harmeyer, July 9, 1975, interview no. 51 a–e, transcript, Oral History of American Music, Yale University, New Haven, Conn.
Marga Richter, videotaped interview by Judith St. Croix, 1987.
Marga Richter, taped telephone interview by Bruce Duffie, July 18, 1996. Transcription by author available on Bruce Duffie's Web site, http://www.kcstudio.com/richter2.html.
Marga Richter, taped interview by author, February 22–23, 2005.
Marga Richter, taped interview by author, June 13–14, 2006.
Marga Richter, taped interview by author, May 19, 2011.
Marga Richter, taped interview by author, May 24, 2011.
Marga Richter, taped interview by author, June 7, 2011.
Phyllis Latimer Roberts, taped telephone interview by author, June 2, 2010.
Michael Skelly, taped telephone interview by author, March 19, 2008.
Gerd Stern, "From Beat Scene Poet to Psychedelic Multimedia Artist in San Francisco and Beyond, 1948–1978," an oral history conducted in 1996 by Victoria Morris Byerly, Regional Oral History Office, the Bancroft Library, University of California, Berkeley, 2001.

http://www.archive.org/stream/beatscenepoetoogerdrich/beatscenepoetoogerdrich_djvu.txt.
Vivian Taylor, taped telephone interview by author, July 13, 2010.

AUDIOCASSETTE TAPES PRIVATELY HELD BY MARGA RICHTER

Interview of MR for Composers Forum, WNYC FM (Richter/Bookspan), 1974–75.
Interview of MR for WFUV, "Blackberry Vines and Winter Fruit," October 11, 1981.
Interview of MR for WBAI; Richter and Others AWC, March 28, 1984.
Interview of MR for WNYC by André Bernard, *Tim Page Show*, January 21, 1985. (Ellen Taaffe Zwilich is also on this tape.)
Interview of MR for WBAI by Jim Theobald, May 29, 1985.
Interview of MR for WKCR by David Soldier, March 6, 1986.
Interview of MR for Morning Pro Musica, "Marga Richter Birthday," 1986.
Interview of MR for WNYC-FM by Tim Page, "New, Old and Unexpected," November 10, 1986.
Interview of MR for Morning Pro Musica, WGBH, "M. Richter and Patricia McCarty violist," March 20, 1987.
Interview of MR for WRHU 88.7 FM, December 9, 1987.
Music for Lecture.

TRANSCRIPTION OF RADIO BROADCAST

David Garland. Remarks on *Evening Music*, WNYC. March 31, 1999.

WEB SITES

Friends of Music at Guilford Presents David Wells. Friday, February 9, 2007. http://ibrattleboro.com/ (accessed May 28, 2009).
Kurt Weill Foundation for Music. http://www.kwf.org/kwf/detailed-chronology-1950–1959 (accessed June 4, 2010).
Leonarda Productions. http://www.leonarda.com/ (accessed June 29, 2008).
The Living Composers Project. http://www.composers21.com/ (accessed June 15, 2008).
The Lortel Archives: The Internet Off-Broadway Database. http://www.lortel.org/lla_archive/ (accessed June 4, 2010).
Marga Richter. Biography at Carl Fischer site. http://www.carlfischer.com/fischer/richterbio.html (accessed July 10, 2010).
Marga Richter. List of Works at Carl Fischer site. http://www.carlfischer.com/fischer/richterworks.html (accessed July 10, 2010).
Marga Richter. Composer's own Web site. http://www.margarichter.com/ (accessed May 27, 2011).

Selected Books, Articles, Dissertations, and Reviews

Ammer, Christine. *Unsung: A History of Women in American Music.* 2nd ed. Portland, Ore.: Amadeus Press, 2001.

Anthony, Michael. "Orchestra Plays Composer's 'Lament.'" *Minneapolis Tribune* (Oct. 22, 1976), 5B.

Babcock, Marguerite. "Does Feminism Drive Women to Drink? Conflicting Themes." *International Journal of Drug Policy* 7, no. 3 (1996). http://www.drugtext.org/library/articles/96734.htm (accessed January 5, 2011).

Barnes, Clive. "Modern Dance: Harkness Ballet Presents." *New York Times*, November 4, 1967.

———. "Ballet: Hodes's 'Abyss.'" *New York Times*, March 5, 1971, 22.

———. "Ballet: Joffrey's 'Petrushka,' 'Abyss.'" *New York Times*, March 17, 1974.

Battisti, Frank. *The Winds of Change: The Evolution of the Contemporary American Wind Band/Ensemble and Its Conductor*. Galesville, Md.: Meredith Music, 2002.

Brogan, Gretchen. "Composer Marga Richter Was 'Noted' at Age 3." *Minneapolis Star*, October 31, 1961.

Burge, David. "Aaron Copland, Roger Sessions, and the Mid-Century Piano Sonata." In *Twentieth-Century Piano Music*, 185–95. New York: Schirmer, 1990.

Cheek, Lawrence W. "Symphony's 'Landscapes' a Real Triumph." *Tucson Daily Citizen*, March 20, 1976.

Cherry, Robert L. Review of Tucson Symphony Orchestra Concert. *Tucson Tonight*, March 25, 1976.

———. "Tucson Sym: Richter Premiere." *High Fidelity/Musical America*, July 1976.

"Chronik." Düsseldorfer Stadtpost/Düsseldorfer Feuilleton, October 30, 1981.

Close, Roy, M. Review of Minnesota Orchestra Concert. *Minneapolis Star*, October 21, 1976, 12C.

Cohn, Arthur. *The Literature of Chamber Music: Labey to Ronsheim*. Chapel Hill, N.C.: Hinshaw Music, 1997.

Commanday, Robert. "A Triumphant Night for the Oakland Symphony." *San Francisco Chronicle*, April 27, 1978.

Court, Suzanne. Review of *Modern American Classics, Volume 3*, Gerard Schwarz/Czech Radio Symphony Orchestra, MMC 2066, 1998. *Journal for the International Alliance for Women in Music* 6, nos. 1/2 (2000).

Davis, Peter G. "Long Island Composers' Alliance Presents Works of Five Members." *New York Times*, November 29, 1976.

Denton, David. Review of *Modern American Classics, Volume 3*, Gerard Schwarz/Czech Radio Symphony Orchestra, MMC 2066, 1998. *Fanfare*, May/June 1999, 257.

DePinto, Basil. "Women's Philharmonic Premieres Three Works." *Montclarion*, February 11, 1992.

"Dozentenkonzert im Robert-Schumann-Institut: Pathos und Witz." *Rheinische Post*, November 29, 1985.

Ehrenreich, Barbara. "Libation as Liberation?: Going Toe to Toe with Men Is a Feminist Act; Going Drink for Drink with Them Isn't." *Time.com* (2002), under "Women and Drinking/Viewpoint." http://www.time.com/time/2002/wdrinking/viewpoint.html (accessed January 5, 2011).

Ellis, Stephen. "The Want List 1991." *Fanfare* 15, no. 2, (November/December 1991).

Foulkes-Levy, Laurdella, and Burt J. Levy. *Journeys through the Life and Music of Nancy Van de Vate*. Lanham, Md.: Scarecrow Press, 2005.

Frankenstein, Alfred. Review of *M-G-M Records Presents Marga Richter: Lament for Strings*, E3422. *San Francisco Chronicle*, December 1956.
———. "Premiere by Little Symphony." *San Francisco Chronicle*, December 12, 1957.
Fried, Alexander. "Four Numbers, One Standout: 'Abyss' Is Best of Ballet." *San Francisco Examiner*, October 8, 1966, 13.
Fürst-Heidtmann, Monika. "Komponieren als emotionale Notwendigkeit: Ein Porträt der Amerikanischen Komponistin Marga Richter" (Composing as emotional necessity: a portrait of American composer Marga Richter). *Neuland* (Germany) 4 (1983084): 268–76.
Goodman, Peter. "Quintets of Quick Quips, Quintessentially Quirky." *Newsday*, April 22, 1992, 71.
———. "L. I. Composer's Opera Finally Arrives." *Newsday*, December 4, 2002.
Harman, Carter. "Forum Hears Music by Richter, Sokoloff." *New York Times*, Feb. 5, 1951, 18.
Harvey, John. "'Lament' Triggers Longing for Contemporary Richter." *St. Paul Pioneer Press*, October 25, 1976, C10.
Henry, Derrick. "Composer Richter Blends Ideas of Art, Music." *Atlanta Journal: The Atlanta Constitution*, March 20, 1986, D4.
———. "Atlanta Symphony, Soloist Shine in Difficult Piano Concerto." *Atlanta Journal: The Atlanta Constitution*, March 22, 1986.
Hertelendy, Paul. "Conductor Calvin Simmons: Musical to the Core." *Oakland (Calif.) Tribune*, April 27, 1978.
———. "'Ghosts' Was Only Chance for Women's Philharmonic." *San Jose (Calif.) Mercury News*, February 3, 1992.
Hinely, Mary Brown. "Report on the Fourth International Congress on Women in Music." *International Congress on Women in Music Newsletter* 3, nos. 3 & 4 (1986): 1, 4–5.
Hinson, Maurice. *Guide to the Pianist's Repertoire.* 3rd ed. Bloomington: Indiana University Press, 2000.
Houk, Norman. "Nee, Civic Orchestra Open Season." *Minneapolis Tribune*, October 30, 1961.
Hughes, Allen. "Composers Series Opens at Modern." *New York Times*, September 7, 1975.
———. "Concert: The Juilliard's Philharmonia in Festival." *New York Times*, February 5, 1981.
Jezic, Diane. *Women Composers: The Lost Tradition Found.* 2nd ed. Prepared by Elizabeth Wood. New York: Feminist Press, 1994.
Johnson, Tom. "Marga Richter: Good Taste Is Tuneless." *Village Voice*, September 22, 1975, 111.
Jones, Abe D., Jr. "Faculty Trio Performs Story of Faith Found." *News and Record*, July 4, 1997, B7.
Kosman, Joshua. "A Pioneer Theme for Philharmonic." *San Francisco Chronicle*, February 3, 1992.
LaFave, Ken. "'Landscapes' to World Premiere Here." *Arizona Daily Star*, March 17, 1976.
———. "'Landscapes' Premiere Shows Vital Musical Ideas.'" *Arizona Daily Star*, March 20, 1976.

LaForgia, John. "'Fluid, Surreal': Symphony Presents Contemporary Works." *Green Valley (Ariz.) News*, March 20, 1976.

Lee, You Ju. "Marga Richter: A Biographical Sketch and Study of Her Piano Works with Emphasis on Sonata for Piano." DMA diss., University of Georgia, 2000.

———. "Marga Richter's Character Sketches for piano." *Clavier Companion* 3, no. 6 (November/December 2011): 20–27.

LePage, Jane Weiner. *Women Composers, Conductors, and Musicians of the Twentieth Century: Selected Biographies*. Vol. 1. Metuchen, N.J.: Scarecrow Press, 1980.

Libbey, Theodore, Jr. Review of Sunday concert: Marga Richter, Merkin Concert Hall. *New York Times*, October 21, 1981.

Lorraine, Renée Cox. "Recovering Jouissance: Feminist Aesthetics and Music." In *Women and Music: A History*, 2nd ed., edited by Karin Pendle, 3–18. Bloomington: Indiana University Press, 2001.

"Marga Richter's *Sieben Lieder*," *Düsseldorfer Nachrichten*, November 29, 1985.

Milbouer, Staci. "Composer Draws on Roots in Writing Concerto." *Nashua (N.H.) Telegraph*, July 26, 1987, H4.

Miller, David H. Review of *Richter: Concerto for Piano and Violas, Cellos and Basses*, MGM E 3547. *American Record Guide*, December 1957.

Mirchandani, Sharon. "The Choral Music of Marga Richter." *Choral Journal* (May 2003): 9–17.

———. "Marga Richter." In *Women of Influence in Contemporary Music: Nine American Composers*, edited by Michael K. Slayton, 357–404. Lanham, Md.: Scarecrow Press, 2011.

Olmstead, Andrea. *Juilliard: A History*. Urbana: University of Illinois Press, 1999.

Persichetti, Vincent. *Twentieth-Century Harmony*. New York: W. W. Norton, 1961.

Putnam, Thomas. "'Women in Music'—A Promising Start." *Buffalo News*, July 20, 1986.

Rosen, Judith. "Richter, Marga." In *New Grove Dictionary of Women Composers*, edited by Julie Anne Sadie and Rhian Samuel, 389–90. New York: Macmillan, 1994.

Sherman, John K. "Civic Orchestra Displays Increasing Sophistication." *Minneapolis Star*, November 3, 1961.

Simon, Jeff. "Philharmonic to Spotlight Five Composers." *Buffalo Evening News*, May 29, 1975, 2:30.

Sterne, Lawrence. Review of *Concerto for Piano, Violas, Celli and Basses and Aria and Toccata*. *Argonaut*, September 27, 1957.

Taylor, Vivian. "Richter, Marga." In *Women and Music in America Since 1900: An Encyclopedia*, edited by Kristine H. Burns, 2:570–71. Westport, Conn.: Greenwood Press, 2002.

Uhrig, James. "For Marga Richter, Family First and Music Second." *Arizona Daily Wildcat*, Wednesday, March 24, 1976, 8.

———. "Richter 'Landscapes of the Mind' Gets Cool Reception at Music Hall." *Arizona Daily Wildcat*, March 24, 1976.

Van Gelder, L. "For a Composer, a Week of Special Note." *New York Times*, April 9, 1978.

Von Gunden, Heidi. *The Music of Vivian Fine*. Lanham, Md.: Scarecrow Press, 1999.

Wagner, David. "Symphony Salutes Prager in One of Best Concerts This Season." *Madison (Wisc.) Capital Times*, February 2, 1976.

Walsh, Michael. “A Young Conductor with Two Styles.” *San Francisco Examiner*, April 26, 1978.
Wayne, Elsbet. “Berkshire Symphony in Finale.” *Entertainment*, April 1986.
Wilson, G. B. L. “Harkness Ballet in France.” *Dance News*, April 1965, 14.
Zakariasen, Bill. “Jerseyans Feature New Work by Women.” *New York Daily News*, June 20, 1981, 13.

INDEX

Page numbers in *italics* refer to illustrations

SHARON MIRCHANDANI is a professor of music history and theory at Westminster Choir College of Rider University in Princeton, New Jersey.

WOMEN COMPOSERS

Kaija Saariaho
Pirkko Moisala
Marga Richter
Sharon Mirchandani

The University of Illinois Press
is a founding member of the
Association of American University Presses.

Designed by Copenhaver Cumpston
Composed in 9.5/13 Janson
with Meta display
by Barbara Evans
at the University of Illinois Press
Manufactured by Sheridan Books, Inc.

University of Illinois Press
1325 South Oak Street
Champaign, IL 61820-6903
www.press.uillinois.edu